Knife Edge

MALORIE BLACKMAN

Level 4

Retold by Karen Holmes
Series Editors: Andy Hopkins and Jocelyn Potter

Pearson Education Limited
Edinburgh Gate, Harlow,
Essex CM20 2JE, England
and Associated Companies throughout the world.

ISBN: 978-1-4082-9138-2

This edition first published by Pearson Education Ltd 2013

1 3 5 7 9 10 8 6 4 2

Original copyright © Oneta Malorie Blackman 2004
Text copyright © Pearson Education Ltd 2013
Illustrations by 171 Jonathan

Set in 11/14pt Bembo
Printed in China
SWTC/01

Published by Pearson Education Limited in association with
Penguin Books Ltd, and both companies being subsidiaries of Pearson PLC

Contents

Introduction

'Roxie told me who you are,' Jaxon said. 'I didn't recognise you.
I didn't realise you were one of us.'
Us and them. Them and us. Always the same. Nothing changed.
Jaxon looked down at you, Callie, and his face showed his surprise.
You're too light to be a Cross and too dark to be all nought.

In a society where people are judged by their colour, the dark-skinned Crosses hold all the power. Sephy, an eighteen-year-old Cross, has given birth to a mixed-race daughter, Callie Rose. The baby's father, Callum, was a light-skinned nought freedom fighter, but he is dead. Now Sephy must bring up their child alone.

She goes to live in a nought area with Callum's mother and gets a job as a singer in a band, but life is hard. Sephy also knows that Callum's brother, Jude, blames her for all his family's troubles. He wants to destroy her and her baby. Can Sephy protect her child – or will Jude, and her own deep sadness, ruin both their lives?

Knife Edge is the second book by Malorie Blackman about ordinary people whose lives are destroyed by society's treatment of difference. It follows the highly successful *Noughts and Crosses*, which ended with Callum's death and Sephy's pregnancy.

Noughts and Crosses, which is also a Penguin Reader, began the story of Callum and Sephy, a young couple who fell in love.

Sephy – Persephone – was the daughter of a politician, Kamal Hadley. Her mother, Jasmine, drank too much and Sephy's relationship with her older sister, Minerva, was difficult. Her closest friend was Callum McGregor, a nought and the son of one of the Hadleys' employees. After Meggie

McGregor lost her job with the Hadleys, Sephy and Callum continued to meet in secret. Slowly, they fell in love.

Callum's brother, Jude, and their father wanted to change the unequal relationship between noughts and Crosses, so they became members of a terrorist group, the Freedom Fighters. Their anger with the Crosses increased after Callum's older sister, Lynette, killed herself. Many years earlier, a group of nought men had attacked Lynette because she had a Cross boyfriend; the attack had damaged her mind.

Jude and his father, Ryan, were accused of organising a bomb attack on a shopping centre by the Freedom Fighters. Jude ran away, but Ryan was caught and nearly hanged. In the end, he was sent to prison for the rest of his life, but died a few days later while – it seemed – trying to escape.

The McGregor family was destroyed by this event, and Callum lost contact with Jude, who was hiding from the authorities. Callum and Sephy spent one night together before she was sent away to school for two and a half years. During that time she didn't hear from him.

Against his mother's wishes, Callum also joined the Freedom Fighters and he met his brother again. Their small cell was ordered to kidnap Sephy and to demand money from her father for her return. Callum sent her a letter inviting her to a meeting at a beach, where Jude and the others took her prisoner. When Andrew Dorn, assistant to the leader of the Freedom Fighters, came to look at the prisoner, Sephy recognised him as a visitor to her family home. Then, when some members of the cell tried to collect the money for Sephy, they were caught by the police.

Although Sephy was hurt by Callum's part in the kidnap plan, she still loved him. While they were alone together, Callum said that he still loved her too, and they slept together. Finally, he helped her to escape – and she told him that Dorn was a spy, working for the Cross government.

For the next six months, Jude and Callum hid separately from the police. When Callum heard on the radio that Sephy had become pregnant while she was a prisoner, he went secretly to her house. There, he was discovered and arrested. Sephy's father told her that she could save Callum's life by ending her pregnancy, but she refused. Just before the authorities hanged him, Callum heard Sephy's voice in the crowd, shouting that she loved him.

Sephy later gave birth to a daughter, Callie Rose, and their story continues in this book.

Malorie Blackman has written two more books, *Checkmate* and *Double Cross*, that continue the story in *Knife Edge*. She has written more than fifty books and plays, and has won many prizes. Her work is read by young people and adults across the world and she was the first black British writer to sell more than a million books.

In an interview, Malorie Blackman said that she presented the world as black and white in these books because most children and young adults view the world in that way – seeing right and wrong, good and bad. As Sephy gets older, she begins to realise that life is not so simple, and she is forced to grow up. But in *Knife Edge*, Sephy is still trying to find her way in an unforgiving world ...

DAILY SHOUTER

Thursday 28 January

Government Minister's Daughter Shot

DAILY SHOUTER

Wednesday 12 May

Nought Terrorist Shot Dead

Chapter 1   A New Beginning?

Jude

Jude, my feet hurt,' Morgan complained. 'I've been watching the traffic for the last three hours.'

'Just keep looking out of the window,' I said from my bed in our hotel room. 'We don't want any surprises.'

Morgan moved the curtain again so he could look at the street below. I turned on the TV, but my mind was on other things.

I was thinking about Andrew Dorn. He was an assistant to the head of the Freedom Fighters – but he was also working for the Crosses. He'd betrayed my cell. Because of him, our kidnap of Sephy Hadley had gone badly wrong. Because of him, every member of my Freedom Fighters cell had been killed or caught – except Morgan and me. Andrew Dorn was working closely with Kamal Hadley, a Cross government minister, and Hadley hated everything about noughts like me. That was why we'd decided to kidnap his daughter Sephy. But the whole operation was a disaster – because of Andrew Dorn.

And I had no idea where he was or how to reach him.

Since my brother Callum's death, nothing had gone right. The police offered large cash rewards to anyone who gave them information about us. The newspapers called us terrorists. We weren't. We were just fighting for what was right. Noughts were second-class citizens. What was it about our lighter skin that made the Crosses afraid of us?

The Cross authorities had made a big mistake killing my brother. Every night before I slept, and every morning when I woke up, I made a promise. I promised my brother to punish every person who was responsible for his death.

But the Freedom Fighters were running from the authorities.

'Something's happening,' Morgan said from the window.

So here we were – Morgan and I – in a cheap hotel in a bad part of town. After months of silence when we didn't hear from our commanders, we'd finally received our orders. We had to book into Room 14 and wait. After two days, we were still waiting.

'Something's happening,' Morgan said from the window. 'There are two ... no, three police cars. How did they know we were here?'

'We'll worry about that later when we're out of here,' I told him. Had somebody betrayed us to the police? Was this more of Andrew Dorn's work?

We ran down the hall to the fire exit. Morgan pulled open the door and we started to run down the stairs. Below us came the sound of feet running up to meet us. I pointed upwards. Morgan and I turned and ran up the stairs instead of down.

'Follow me,' Morgan whispered. He was responsible for our escape plans.

I followed him down a hall to Room 25. As he knocked on the door, I put my hand on the gun in my jacket pocket. Nobody was going to hang me.

The door opened almost immediately and Morgan ran inside. A strong, middle-aged Cross man with a moustache and short hair stood in the middle of the room, watching us. I couldn't hear anyone following us.

'They've gone to our room on the first floor,' I whispered to Morgan. He nodded. I was surprised that he hadn't pulled out his gun. The Cross man was still watching us, but he didn't look frightened. 'We've got to get out of here,' I told him.

'You'll pretend to be my driver and my secretary,' said the Cross.

'Is that OK with you, Boss?' Morgan asked me.

I looked carefully at the Cross and nodded. So he was going

to help us, was he? He was part of Morgan's escape plan. I had a rule:

Never trust a Cross. Ever.

'I'm Dylan Hoyle,' said the Cross. He held out his hand, but I didn't take it. 'OK,' he continued. 'You've both worked for me for the last eighteen months. Your false papers are in my jacket pocket.' He took out the papers and handed them to us. 'Make yourselves look like the photos on the documents. There are clothes, glasses and hats in the cupboard.'

Morgan and I were having to rely on a Cross. I didn't want to do that, but I had no choice.

We changed out of our usual uniform of jeans and shirts. I put on a cheap blue suit. Morgan wore dark grey trousers and a long raincoat.

'I'll take back the papers,' said Dylan. 'Walk behind me. Don't speak without looking at me first for permission. Is that clear?'

Morgan gave his papers back immediately and nodded. It was harder for me. I *gave* orders – I didn't take them.

'If you want to live, you'll obey me,' Dylan said to me.

'OK,' I said angrily. 'Let's do this. But Dylan, if you try to betray us, *you* won't live.'

Dylan went to the door first. He walked calmly out of the room towards the lift in the middle of the hall, with Morgan and me a couple of steps behind him. The lift arrived and we all stepped in. Dylan pressed the button for the underground car park at the back of the hotel.

As the lift moved quickly down, my heart began to beat a little louder, a little faster. My gun had fourteen bullets and there were more in my pockets. Meggie McGregor didn't give birth to any stupid children – just unlucky ones.

'Take your hands out of your pockets,' Dylan told me without turning his head.

The lift doors opened. We walked out into the car park

behind Dylan. We had no idea what was going to happen next.

'Excuse me, sir.' A dagger★ policeman came running up to us. Another policeman stood just a few metres behind him, his gun already in his hand.

'Yes, officer?' Dylan stepped in front of me and Morgan. 'Can I help you?'

'We're looking for two nought terrorists. We think they're staying in this hotel,' said the officer. 'Have you seen anyone suspicious?'

'No!' Dylan replied, looking shocked.

The officer stepped around Dylan and looked at Morgan and me, then at the photo of us in his hand. Somebody in the Freedom Fighters had sent us to the hotel, then told the police. Andrew Dorn.

'And you are ...?' the officer asked me.

'This is Ben, my driver, and that's John Halliwell, my secretary,' Dylan said.

'I see,' said the officer. He turned back to me. 'Can I see your documents, please? Yours as well,' he said to Morgan.

'When they're with me, I keep their papers, officer,' said Dylan. 'In my experience, that keeps them under my control.'

The officer smiled as Dylan gave the papers to him. He looked at them and handed them back.

'That's OK, sir,' said the police officer. 'You can go.'

'Thank you, officer,' Dylan said confidently, one Cross to another. He walked calmly out to a big black car on the road. Then he threw the key at me and waited.

Why is he looking at me? I wondered. Then I understood. I tried not to show my anger as I opened the back door of the car for him.

★ dagger/blanker: In this book, these are very rude words for a Cross and a nought. In normal English, a dagger is a sharp knife that can kill someone. A blank is an empty space.

I climbed into the driving seat. Morgan sat next to me. I started the engine and we drove away. We drove past police cars on both sides of the road. After five minutes, Dylan started giving me directions until we turned into a supermarket car park.

'This is where we say goodbye,' Dylan said when I'd stopped the car.

'Thanks for helping us, Dylan,' Morgan said. 'I'll see you again.'

Dylan nodded at me, but I didn't look at him. I didn't want to talk to a dagger. When he'd driven away, I turned to Morgan.

'When did you become so friendly with a Cross?'

'Dylan is a contact I made a few years ago, before you joined the Freedom Fighters. I've put him or other friendly Crosses in all the hotels we've stayed in over the last few months.'

I was annoyed by the thought that a dagger had helped us to escape. 'I don't like using daggers. You can't trust any of them.'

'Jude, sometimes we have to trust Crosses,' said Morgan. 'I don't know about you, but I'm in the Freedom Fighters to fight for equality. What's *your* reason? Are you using the Freedom Fighters to punish every Cross that you meet?'

'I'm not going to answer that question,' I said angrily. 'We have more urgent matters to discuss. Who told the police that we were at the hotel?'

'I've been thinking about that too,' Morgan said. 'I think it was Dorn. He must really want to hurt us.'

'That makes him even more dangerous,' I said. 'The police know that we're together, so we need to separate. I'll use my phone to contact you.'

'Dorn has to pay for what he did to us,' Morgan said. 'Your brother was hanged because of him ...'

'Dorn wasn't responsible for Callum's death – or only partly.

My brother died because of Persephone Hadley,' I said coldly.

Morgan couldn't understand how much I hated Sephy Hadley and all daggers. But mainly Sephy Hadley. Everything began with her and my brother. Now Callum was gone and Sephy was going to suffer. I intended to destroy her.

♦

Sephy
Dearest Callie,

When I first held you in my arms, I waited to feel something. Anything. And nothing came. No pleasure. No pain. No love. I didn't know you. I looked at you and you were a stranger.

Then I started to feed you. I realised in that moment how much I didn't know about you, Callie. You're a real person, someone who relies on me for everything. I felt so frightened. You're my daughter and I'm responsible for you.

Tears ran down my cheeks. I smiled at you and I was sure that you smiled back. Just a little smile, but that was all I needed. I watched you feed with your eyes closed and one hand resting against my skin. You lay on my chest and you slept.

I closed my eyes too, but then Nurse Fashoda tried to take you from me. My eyes opened immediately.

'What are you doing?'

'I'm putting your baby in the cot at the end of your bed. You need to rest.'

'Can't she sleep on my chest?'

'Our beds are too narrow. She might fall off. She can sleep with you when you're home in your own big bed.' Her voice was cold. Why was she so angry with me? 'Look around,' she said. 'This is a small local hospital. We don't get half the equipment or the doctors and nurses that a Cross hospital receives. Not many Cross patients want to come here. When you leave, you'll move back into your expensive house and you'll forget about us.'

From one look at the colour of my skin, Nurse Fashoda thought she knew my life history. She didn't know anything about me. The bed in my flat was narrower than the one I was lying on. The bedroom, bathroom and kitchen together were the size of this small hospital ward.

I was too tired to argue with her. But as soon as she left the room, I moved down to the bottom of the bed to look at you. I touched your cheek. I couldn't take my eyes off you.

Later, I watched the other mothers welcome their loved ones – husbands, partners, parents. Every bed had at least one visitor – except mine.

I'm writing this as you sleep in the cot at the bottom of my bed. We've been together for a few hours now and I can't stop looking at you. I can't believe that you're mine.

I can't stop thinking about your father, Callum, either. I miss him. Now there's just you and me against the world.

There's so much that I want to say to you. It frightens me how much I already care about you. When I was pregnant, I hated you because you were alive and Callum was dead. I hated you and myself and the whole world. But now that you're here, I feel the beginning of peace.

I sit on my hospital bed and look down at you. You have your dad's eyes – the same shape – but yours are dark blue and his were grey. You have my nose, strong and proud – but you don't look like either of us. Your skin's much lighter brown than mine, but you're not a nought, not white like your dad. Maybe you're the hope for the future. Something new and different and special.

But I worry about you. You have to live in a world separated into noughts and Crosses, where you are neither. Don't let people tell you who or what you are. Be yourself. Find your own place and space and time. Callie, I want to surround you with love. I want you to know about your dad. How he made me laugh and cry more than anyone else. I loved him so much. He isn't here, but you are and I'll never let anything or anyone hurt you.

Before I had you, I was a peace-loving person. But now my feelings have changed. For you, I would die. I would kill to protect you. I won't let anyone hurt you. No one.

My feelings frighten me. I loved Callum with all my heart too, and my love for him brought us terrible pain. Love is bad luck. And now I'm lying in the hospital feeling sorry for myself because Callum's not with me. *You're* here with me, Callie Rose, but I miss your father.

With every heartbeat, I miss him.

Chapter 2   Jude Meets a Girl and Sephy Makes Plans

Jude

I sat opposite Mum's house in my stolen car for a long time, watching and waiting. I wanted to see if she was all right. Did she know how much I missed her?

The whole situation was crazy. I had no friends and no home. I didn't feel safe in the Freedom Fighters – not when Andrew Dorn was still an important member. My life was a mess. That was how it felt. But then I remembered my brother hanging, dying ...

My brother Callum. He was the member of my family who was going to be a success. He had everything – and it killed him. If *he* couldn't succeed, what hope was there for the rest of us?

I wanted to tell Mum that I hadn't forgotten her. Did she get the money that I sent her? It wasn't much, and not every week, but I tried to help her. I couldn't knock on her door. I was wanted by the government, the police and some people in the Freedom Fighters. But I was still alive, and I was still thinking about her.

Then her door opened and she came out with a rubbish bag. She looked so old and bent!

Suddenly, she looked up at me. She called my name, dropped her bag and ran towards me. I had to drive away before somebody heard her. *Mum,* I thought, *please don't cry. It was a mistake to come here. I'm so sorry.* I'd broken my own rule:

Never ever allow yourself to feel. Feelings kill.

After I left Mum's house, I went to the Golden Eye bar. It wasn't my usual sort of place, but it was hidden away. It was busy, mostly with noughts but there were quite a few daggers.

I was tired of running and hiding. I needed to get some purpose back into my life. First, I needed money – lots of it and quickly.

'Hi. Is this seat taken?'

I looked up at the Cross woman standing in front of me. Couldn't she find somewhere else to sit? Then I saw two police officers enter the bar – a nought and a Cross.

'Sit down,' I said quickly. I forced myself to smile at her.

'Thanks,' she said as she sat down. 'I'm Cara.'

'Steve,' I lied.

'Hi, Steve,' Cara the Cross continued. 'This place is busy tonight.'

I didn't want to talk to her or sit next to her. But I smiled and was careful to keep my true feelings off my face. I looked quickly around the room. The police officers had papers in their hands.

'So, Cara,' I smiled, moving closer. 'Do you work near here?'

'Yes, in the hair salon around the corner. It's mine. I own seven salons around the country.'

So she had money. That was useful. The police officers were only a table away now, showing photos to the customers.

The police officers were only a table away now ...

Were they the photos of Morgan and me?

'You're very beautiful,' I whispered to Cara.

And I kissed her, feeling sick in my stomach. The police walked past me. It took all my strength not to pull away from Cara until they were gone.

'I hope that didn't offend you,' I said. 'I couldn't stop myself.' I smiled and took a drink of my beer to wash away the taste of her lips. 'Can I get you a drink?'

She was probably just being friendly when she spoke to me at first, but then she'd let me kiss her. She didn't try to stop me. I knew what kind of stupid Cross woman she was.

I went to the bar. When my back was towards her, I cleaned my mouth with the back of my hand. Then I returned with the drinks.

'After your drink, do you want to get out of here?' I suggested. 'We could watch a film, go for a walk, or maybe you could show me your salon.'

Cara looked at me carefully. 'OK,' she said, after a moment.

This was the opportunity I needed. I had to get money, and Cara was going to give it to me – whether she wanted to or not.

We went to the cinema. Cara chose an awful romantic film and cried through the last ten minutes of it. I thought about her seven salons and her money. I put my arm around her and she immediately put her head on my shoulder.

Afterwards we went for a meal and I took her home. She didn't invite me in, but she wanted to see me again.

'I'll give you my phone number,' she said. I could feel her embarrassment as she handed it to me, then almost ran from the gate to her front door.

'Cara?' I called after her. 'I'll see you soon.'

She nodded and I'm sure I saw hope on her face. I watched her go into the house before I walked away. If I wanted her money, I had to play my cards right. But I wasn't worried. Another of my rules is:

Do to others as they will do to you – but do it first.

♦

Sephy

Dearest Callie,

Please, *please* don't go. I don't know what I'll do if I lose you too. They took you away from me and put you in the Special Care Baby Ward because you were having trouble breathing and you were losing weight. I can't afford to take you to a private hospital with better equipment. When I left home, Dad stopped giving me money. I can't ask him for help, and I don't want to ask Mother. I felt helpless when they took you from me, exactly like I did on the day that Callum was killed.

Now the doctors have told me that you're starting to get stronger. You can come back to the ward, but we can't leave hospital until you're eating well and weigh more. That's OK. As I watch and wait, I'm making plans. I want to make a good life for both of us. I haven't got any money, but I want to get a job and work hard. I'm only eighteen; I can go back to school later. First, I want to look after you and make you happy.

I'm in no hurry to go back to my flat. I didn't go home to my mother after Callum died. I couldn't – that was my old life. You're my new life, the future. Callum's still in my thoughts all the time. I don't want to forget about him. But you must get better – that's the most important thing.

Chapter 3   Jude Falls in Love and Sephy Has Visitors

Jude

I put on my cleanest clothes and my leather jacket. Half

an hour later, I was standing outside Cara's hair salon. It was the middle of the morning and the place was full. I wondered whether to go in, but I needed money and a place to stay. Cara could give me both.

Cara came to the door when she saw me, a big smile on her face.

'I hope it's OK for me to come here,' I said.

'Yes, of course. I'm glad to see you.'

'I've got some tickets for a film. Do you want to come with me.'

'I'd love to, but we close late tonight,' said Cara sadly. 'I don't finish work until after nine, and then I have to lock up the shop.'

'Well,' I said, 'it was just an idea.' Maybe this wasn't going to be so easy.

'Why don't I cook a late dinner for us at my house?' said Cara. 'I warn you, though, I'm not a very good cook.'

'I am,' I said truthfully. 'I'll do the cooking.'

I arranged to meet her at the salon at nine o'clock. As I left, I turned back and waved. Stupid, stupid woman. She'd invited me to her house, but she didn't know me. Cara was going to learn not to trust people so easily.

At nine o'clock, I was standing outside the darkened salon but she wasn't there. At that moment, she was probably laughing with her friends about me ... I wanted to hit her.

'Steve? STEVE!'

I turned. Cara was running up the road towards me.

'I thought I was going to miss you,' she said. 'I went to the bank to put the money in the night safe. I don't like leaving it in the salon,' she explained.

She did most of the talking as I walked with her to her home. She talked about the salon and how both noughts and Crosses used it. I wasn't really listening.

'I'm probably boring you,' Cara said.

Yes, you are, I thought. But I said, 'Of course not. You love your work and it shows. There's nothing wrong with that.'

'You're really nice, Steve.' Cara smiled at me gratefully.

The warmth of her smile made me feel ... uncomfortable, which I didn't expect. We arrived at her house. It was the first time I'd visited a dagger's house since I was a child. It was strange and it didn't feel safe.

I started to prepare the food that she'd bought. Suddenly, I felt her watching me.

'Is something wrong?' I asked.

'I'm just wondering about you,' Cara said thoughtfully. 'Am I right about you? Are you as lonely as I am?'

I stopped moving. At first I couldn't answer, then I said, 'Yes, you're right. I've got no one.'

I'd never said that before. And who was the first person to hear it? A dagger. I closed my eyes and looked away. I hated her for realising that I was lonely. When the time was right, I'd punish her for that.

But she surprised me by kissing me on the cheek. I stared at her and then she moved away. I think we were both embarrassed.

We ate dinner and listened to music, talked and laughed. And all the time I tried not to look into her eyes for too long. I tried not to relax or smile or touch her.

Almost three hours later, Cara walked with me to the door.

'Thank you,' I said. 'I've really enjoyed myself.'

'I have too,' said Cara. 'I hope we can do it again some time.'

I opened the door and stepped out into the night. I couldn't wait to leave. The whole evening was an uncomfortable mistake – because I'd enjoyed it too much. I reminded myself why I was with her. I had to spend time with a dagger to get money for the Freedom Fighters. She was just a dagger woman – and all daggers deserved punishment.

But my evening with Cara was the best that I'd spent in a long time. It was relaxing and pleasant and it showed me all the things I'd missed – not just for months, but for years. There was a calmness about Cara that allowed me to relax. But I couldn't let down my defences, not for Cara or anyone.

Never ever allow yourself to feel. Feelings kill.

♦

Sephy

Dearest Callie,

My sister Minerva visited us today. I hadn't had any other visitors and I wasn't expecting any.

'Hello, Sephy.'

'Hello, Minerva.' Several seconds passed as we looked at each other.

'How's your arm?' I asked at last. Your Uncle Jude, your dad's brother, shot your Aunt Minerva in the arm when I was six months pregnant. He hates my whole family, but especially me.

The wait in the hospital after she was shot was awful. I didn't know whether she would lose her arm – or her life. But when she woke up, I asked her not to report Jude to the police.

'Tell them that an unknown attacker came into my flat,' I said to her. 'Tell them that when I refused to give him money, he shot you and ran away.'

Minerva didn't want to lie. She wanted Jude to pay for his actions and I did too. But I didn't want people to start talking about the McGregors and the Hadleys again. I didn't want reporters on my doorstep. I didn't want to hurt Jude's mum. Finally Minerva agreed, but afterwards our relationship changed.

Stay away from Jude, Callie. He wants me to suffer. I'm

not frightened of him, but I'm frightened that he'll use you to hurt me.

'My arm's fine,' Minerva said. 'Can I have a look at my niece?'

'She's down there.' I pointed to the cot at the bottom of the bed. Minerva looked down at you. Finally she said, 'Hello, baby.'

'Why are you here, Minerva? You didn't want to see me after you were shot. Why now?'

'I was angry and blamed you for what happened to me. Then after I came out of hospital, you'd disappeared. No one knew where you were.'

What could I say to her? That I was living in a small, cold flat and that I had no money?

'Why didn't you come home after ... after what happened with Jude?' she asked.

'It isn't my home now.'

'Yes it is. We all want you to come back. Mother and I miss you.'

'How is Mother?' I asked. 'Is she still drinking too much?'

'No,' Minerva said, to my surprise. 'After Dad left, I thought she'd start again. But I don't think she's missing him. She's too busy thinking about you and what's gone wrong between you.'

'Have you left home yet?'

'No. I don't want to leave Mother alone.' She looked down at her watch. 'I have to go. Sephy, is it ... is it OK for Mother to visit?'

'If she wants to visit, I can't stop her. But tell her not to criticise Callum. Where are you hurrying to?'

'A job interview at the *Daily Shouter*. I'm going to be a journalist.'

Our relationship has always been difficult, but I care about her. And I think she cares about me.

'Good luck,' I said.

'Thanks. And Sephy – you have a beautiful daughter.'

Later that day, I started talking to Roxie, the woman in the next bed. She'd given birth to a son a few hours earlier. I was putting you back in her cot when Roxie smiled at me.

'Your daughter's very beautiful,' she said.

'I think so,' I replied. Lots of people were hurrying into the ward. 'Are you expecting visitors?'

'I'm not sure. My husband is working.' Then she smiled. 'Oh! Here's my brother, Jaxon.'

I looked down the ward and watched a tall man with shoulder-length fair hair walk towards us, with a guitar on his back. He didn't look much older than me.

'Hi, Sister!' Jaxon kissed Roxie's cheek before picking up his nephew.

'Jaxon, this is Sephy. Sephy, this is Jaxon Robbins, my brother.'

He nodded quickly at me. His attention was on his family. 'What's the sprog's name, then?'

'*Sprog*?' I said. 'I've never heard that word before.'

'It's a nought word for a child. Not everything in our lives is controlled by Crosses. We noughts need to keep something for ourselves.' Jaxon looked straight at me for the first time.

'Jaxon, stop it,' Roxie said angrily. 'Sephy, I'm sorry about him.'

'Don't worry,' I said. 'I prefer people to be honest.'

I moved down to the cot and picked you up. Out of the corner of my eye, I saw Roxie whisper something to her brother. He looked at me, then he came over to me.

'Roxie told me who you are,' Jaxon said. 'I didn't recognise you. I didn't realise you were one of us.'

Us and them. Them and us. Always the same. Nothing changed.

Jaxon looked down at you, Callie, and his face showed his surprise. You're too light to be a Cross and too dark to be all nought.

'Where do you play that?' I asked, pointing at the guitar.

'I play any time, any place, anywhere,' he replied.

After looking up and down the ward, I said, 'Why don't you play a song now, to make us all more cheerful?'

I was joking but Jaxon immediately said, 'Only if you join me!'

He began to play his guitar and started singing. I took a deep breath and sang with him, quietly at first, then louder. Jaxon looked at me, surprised. He had a good voice. Me? At first I worried about forgetting the words, but then I started to enjoy it. We didn't sound so bad. The other people in the ward were actually smiling. But then I saw Nurse Solomon marching up the ward towards us.

'There's no singing in this ward,' she shouted angrily. She tried to take hold of Jaxon's guitar. That was a big mistake.

'Listen, you horrible dagger woman – don't you ever touch my guitar again.' His voice was quiet but frightening.

Nurse Solomon pulled back her hand. Except for some crying babies, the ward was silent. She walked back to her desk at the end of the ward. Jaxon's words hurt – I was a dagger too.

'Sephy, I'm sorry about that,' said Jaxon. 'But I don't let anybody touch my guitar. I didn't mean you.'

'Yes, you did. I'm a Cross too,' I reminded him. 'Now, please excuse me.'

I picked you up, Callie, and waited for him to move back to his sister's bed. I couldn't forget his words.

One of us ... One of them ...

Then guess who came to see me this morning? Mother. I realised, with surprise, that she wasn't drunk and that I was pleased to see her. We hadn't spoken since before Minerva was shot.

She went straight to your cot and smiled slowly. I'd never seen that look on her face before – one of complete love.

'Hello, Callie Rose – and welcome,' Mother said.

A single tear ran down my cheek. I turned my head so she wouldn't see, and brushed it away.

'Sephy, she's so beautiful,' Mother said.

'Yes, she looks like her dad,' I said quietly.

'Yes, she does,' Mother agreed. 'Did you call her Callie for Callum?'

'It was the closest girl's name to his that I could think of.'

'Callie Rose ... It's a lovely name,' said Mother.

This kindness was hurting me. It was easier to fight her.

'Why are you here?' I asked.

She smiled. 'I wanted to see you and my granddaughter,' she said. 'What are your plans for the future?'

'I want to live each day minute by minute. I don't have any other plans,' I told her.

'Minute by minute doesn't work with a baby. You need to plan ahead for your daughter.'

'And when will I stop caring for her like you stopped caring for me?' I asked angrily.

'Sephy, I know I wasn't there when you needed me most. I was a politician's wife. Politics came before everything – including you and Minerva. That was what your father wanted.' She paused. 'Sephy, the past is finished. We have to do what's right for your daughter now. I think you and Callie Rose should come home with me. I want us to be friends again and I want to help with Callie. I want to be part of my granddaughter's life.'

I looked at her. I could see that she meant every word. We'd both said some hurtful things in the past, but I was tired. Was I too tired to hate her? It would be so easy to move in with

20

Mother, and you'd be safe away from Jude …

'Are you still drinking – even sometimes?' I asked.

'I haven't drunk any alcohol since Callum was … killed,' Mother informed me. 'Come home, Sephy. Please.'

'OK.' I nodded. 'I'll come home with you.' I didn't want to ask anyone in my family for help, but I had to think about you.

'You will?' Mother looked so happy that I felt happier too. 'I'll go and get your room ready. It'll be good to have you home.'

Mother kissed me on the cheek, something that she hadn't done for years.

An hour later, I had another visitor, Callum's mum. That was even more of a surprise. I hadn't seen her since before Callum died. What did she want? Did she hate me as much as Jude did?

She sat in the chair at the side of my bed.

'Can I hold her?' she asked, smiling at you. 'She's very beautiful. Thank you for calling her Callie.'

I took a deep breath. 'Meggie … do you blame me for Callum's death?' I asked.

Meggie shook her head. 'No. I never blamed you.'

'Why not? Jude does.'

'Jude is very confused. He blames you and every other Cross for everything that's wrong with his life.' She paused, then said, 'I want to suggest something. You could move into my house and I could help with Callie Rose. We're both alone now, so it would be the best solution. You and Callie are my family now.'

What could I do? I wanted to go home to Mother, but Meggie clearly needed us. Whatever I decided, I'd hurt someone.

'Are you sure you wouldn't mind being kept awake by a crying baby?' I asked.

'I'd love it.' Meggie smiled.

'Then we'll come,' I said. 'But you must let me pay rent and half of the bills.'

I thought she was going to argue, but she didn't. 'OK. I'll come for you tomorrow morning. I'll have a reason to get up in the mornings again with you and my granddaughter in the house.'

Had I made the right decision? I'd soon know.

Chapter 4   Jude Loses his Temper and Sephy Receives a Letter

Jude

I met Cara regularly for the next two weeks. I decided to be patient. I didn't just want one day's money from the local hair salon – I wanted *all* Cara's money, from all the salons. She probably had hundreds of thousands of pounds in the bank. I knew I could get it because she cared about me.

Sometimes when we were talking or laughing together, I forgot that she was a Cross. When that happened, I forced myself to see her skin colour and nothing else. But I knew that I was starting to forget about the differences between us, and that worried me.

I surprised Cara at work one afternoon and we went for a walk, then back to her house for dinner.

'Steve, do you like me?' Cara asked without warning.

I was annoyed. Why did girls always want to talk about relationships and feelings?

'Of course I like you,' I replied.

'Then why have you never done more than kiss me?' Cara asked. She was embarrassed and couldn't look into my eyes.

'I've had a lot to think about recently,' I said. 'I'm looking for a job and I've got bills to pay. Things aren't going very well for me at the moment.'

'Then let me help you. It's only money, Steve.' She went to her desk and opened one of the locked drawers. She took out her cheque book. 'How much do you need?' She was signing a cheque before writing the amount.

'I'm not taking your money,' I told her quietly. 'I think I'd better leave.'

'Steve …' Cara placed a warm hand against my face. Then she kissed me. I closed my eyes and put my arms around her. It was a long time since anyone had cared for me so much. I pulled away.

'What's the matter?' asked Cara.

'Nothing,' I whispered. 'I really have to leave.'

'Steve, I think you're afraid to get close to anyone. Won't you tell me what happened? My dad died − of a heart attack. Have you lost someone important to you too?'

I felt strange, frightened. How did she understand so much about me? At first I couldn't speak, then I said, 'My brother. My brother died … He was murdered.'

Cara nodded. She understood my pain and that was the worst thing. She understood me − completely.

I wanted her to stop talking, stop understanding me. My throat hurt. My eyes hurt. *Stop talking. Stop … STOP …* She was right. I was lonely. I'd been lonely even before my family was destroyed. Why did I always find it hard to get close to people? Why was it impossible for me to make friends and keep them? And why was I now kissing a Cross without wanting to stop?

I pulled her closer. I tried to think about her skin, but I could only see her warm, brown eyes, smiling at me with understanding. With love. *With love.*

I hit her, hard, and her body fell backwards. She looked up at me, too shocked to cry out. Her eyes showed her hurt, but the love was still there. I went down on my knees beside her and hit her again.

And then I couldn't stop. I punched her again and again,

I hit her, hard, and her body fell backwards.

then I stood up and kicked her. I was so angry. Why did she make me care about her? I wanted to show both of us that she meant nothing to me. I hit her harder and harder, even when she was screaming at me to stop.

Finally, she stopped screaming.

But I only stopped when I was too tired to continue. My hands were covered with blood. I cleaned them on my trousers. I picked up the signed cheque from the floor. I went to the drawer and took out her money, cheque book and bank books. Then I left the house. I was careful not to look at Cara. Not once.

My brain cleared. I had money and I was going to cash the cheques early the next morning. Then I was going to disappear. I was good at that.

I'd only walked a few steps when I realised that my face was wet. I looked up. When had it started to rain? The night was bright with a thousand stars, and the air was warm on my face. There wasn't a cloud in the sky.

♦

Sephy
Dearest Callie,

Mother didn't understand my decision. 'You said you were coming home with me,' she reminded me when I phoned her.

'I've changed my plans. Callum's mum said I could stay with her. I've decided to … to live with her instead. She's got no other family.' I knew that I was hurting her. 'I'm sorry, Mother.'

'So you prefer to live in a hut with a nought than come home with me?' asked Mother.

'I prefer not to listen to insults about noughts,' I replied. 'Mother, I don't want to fight with you. I'm too tired. I'll come and see you soon.'

'Goodbye, Persephone,' said Mother. She put down the phone

first – but not before I heard her crying. I wanted to cry too.

So, Callie, here I am at Meggie's house. It's small, but warm and clean and better than my own flat. Meggie sleeps in the small bedroom upstairs and I have the bigger one. We argued about that, but Meggie refused to change her mind.

I phoned Minerva to ask about her new job at the *Daily Shouter*. She was shocked when I told her where I was living.

'But it's a really rough area,' she told me. 'My first job here was to interview a woman a couple of streets away from Meggie's house. On the way back to the office I was attacked.'

'What?' I asked, worried. 'Are you all right? Were you hurt?'

'No. A nought pushed me against a wall. He took my purse and my phone, then ran off.'

'You were unlucky …'

'Sephy, noughts are responsible for most of the crimes in this country. Remember that,' Minerva told me.

'That doesn't mean that every nought is a criminal. I prefer to trust people, noughts and Crosses, until they give me a reason to distrust them.'

'That's why you get hurt,' Minerva said.

I couldn't think of an answer. I changed the subject of our conversation before we started arguing.

'Congratulations on your new job,' I said.

'The newspaper is employing me for six months. If they like my work, they'll keep me. I've reported on a couple of nought attacks on noughts, and a fire. No Crosses were hurt, so they were only small stories.'

'The noughts probably didn't think they were small stories,' I replied. I was shocked by Minerva's words.

We talked for a few more minutes. I learned that Mother was really unhappy, but she hadn't started drinking again. I was pleased about that.

Life isn't easy in Meggie's house. I don't feel completely comfortable and Callie, you cry so much. Sometimes I want to scream at you to stop. I'm always so tired. I think of Callum. I want him to share you with me. Those are the worst times, when I think of him.

One afternoon when you were nearly asleep, the doorbell rang. You immediately started crying again.

'Sephy, it's for you,' Meggie called upstairs.

Annoyed, I carried you downstairs. It was Jaxon, the boy with the guitar that I'd met at the hospital.

'You've come to see me?' I asked, surprised. 'Is something wrong with Roxie?'

'No, she's OK,' said Jaxon. 'Can I sit down?' He looked at me carefully, then he continued, 'You've got a great singing voice. I have a band and we need a female singer. We'd share the money that we make between the four of us.'

I was confused. 'You want me to join your band?'

'Yes. I play guitar, Rhino plays the drums and Sonny plays keyboard. When you sang with me in the hospital, you were good. We'd like you to join us.'

'What kind of places do you play?'

'Clubs, pubs, weddings, parties – anywhere where someone will pay us,' Jaxon told me.

'So why do you want me?' I asked. 'Lots of girls can sing.'

'More Cross clubs will book us if you're our singer,' said Jaxon.

That was honest – Jaxon wanted to use me. I thought about his offer. I wanted to earn some money, but could I sing in front of an audience? And Jaxon had a bad temper and a problem with Crosses. It wouldn't be easy.

'I don't think so,' I said. 'I have a baby to care for.'

'Sephy, you need to spend time out of the house,' said Meggie. 'I love having you and Callie here with me, but I'm worried about you. You don't want to go anywhere or do anything.'

27

I didn't want to argue with her in front of Jaxon. 'Thanks for the offer,' I told him, 'but no.'

He stood up. 'If you change your mind, this is my address and phone number.' He gave me a business card.

Meggie took him to the door. When she came back, she said, 'Sephy, you have to start going out again. You haven't even taken Callie to see your mother yet. And what are you going to do with your life?'

'When Callie is older, I'll think about the future,' I told her.

'How much older?' asked Meggie. 'A month? A year? Ten years? Fifty years? When?'

'Meggie, leave me alone!' I shouted.

I frightened you, Callie, and you started crying again. I ran out of the room with you in my arms. I didn't want to think about the future. I wanted to be with Callum. Why didn't anyone understand that?

Meggie and I didn't say much after that. The next day when the doorbell rang, I let her answer it.

'Sephy, it's for you,' she called upstairs.

I took you downstairs with me. It was a stranger, a Cross man, middle-aged, with grey hair and a moustache. Was he another reporter?

'Yes?' I said coldly. 'Can I help you?'

'My name is Jack. Jack Labinjah. I'm a prison guard. I was with Callum on his last day.'

I suddenly felt very cold and I couldn't breathe.

'You were with Callum …?' I whispered.

'It's taken me a long time to find you. Callum wrote you a letter. I promised to deliver it,' Jack said slowly. 'He wrote more than one letter, actually, but he threw the others away. This is the one he wanted you to have.'

There was an envelope in his hand with my name on the front, in Callum's writing. When I touched it, I felt that

Callum was there, next to me. I could hear his voice in my ear.

'I was with Callum every day until he died,' Jack continued. 'We became good friends. He didn't talk about anything except you.'

'Why couldn't I see him when he was in prison?' I asked.

'We had orders that you couldn't see him,' Jack said.

'Orders from who? The prison governor?' Meggie asked quickly.

'Higher than that,' Jack said softly, looking straight at me.

'It was my dad, wasn't it?'

'Let's sit down and discuss this,' Meggie said.

'I can't.' Jack shook his head. 'I could lose my job for being here, but Callum made me promise. I didn't want to deliver this letter.'

'Why not?' asked Meggie. 'You've read it, haven't you?'

'Yes,' said Jack. 'In my job I can't be too careful.' He looked at me. 'Callum never stopped talking about you. You were the most important person in his life. You need to remember that when you read this.'

'Sephy, I think you should give me that letter,' said Meggie.

'NO!' I shouted. 'It's mine. It's the last thing that Callum sent me. I'm going to hold on to it.'

'I have to go.' Jack was already at the door. 'Miss Hadley, I … I'm sorry.' And then he was gone.

Why was he apologising? I had a gift in my hand that I'd never dreamed of. A letter from Callum. The last letter he'd ever written – and it was to me.

I was shaking when I opened the envelope. I read quickly at first, but more slowly as every word hurt me. When I got to the end, the letter fell from my hands. I turned slowly to Meggie and looked at Callie Rose in her arms.

Our daughter. My daughter. I took her from Meggie, sat down and stared at her. Meggie picked up Callum's letter.

'Don't read it …' I whispered.

She began to read it out loud.

Sephy,

I'm writing this because I want you to know the truth. I don't want you to spend the rest of your life believing a lie.

I don't love you. I never did. You were just a job for me. A way for the Freedom Fighters to get a lot of money from your dad.

You believed everything I said to you. It made me laugh. How could I love someone like you – a Cross and, worse than that, the daughter of one of our worst enemies. I pretended to love you to hurt your parents. And now you're pregnant. I'm really pleased. Now the whole world will know that you're having my child, the child of a blanker.

But no one will know how much I hate you. I feel sick when I think about you and me together.

I've told Jack to deliver this to you when you have our child. I can imagine your face now as you read this. That makes me happy as I wait to die. You'll probably hate me now as much as I hate you.

I don't want you to speak my name ever again. Never tell our child about me. I don't want him or her to know anything about me or how I died. Live your life. You're a Cross, rich, lucky. Someone will always take care of you. Forget about me. I've already forgotten about you.

Callum

Chapter 5   Sephy Joins a Band and Jude Hears Bad News

Sephy

Jaxon's house wasn't hard to find. It was only a twenty-minute walk from Meggie's. It seemed longer, though, because people were staring at me. There weren't many Cross faces in that part of town. And I was already missing Rose. Rose is a much better name for my baby.

Callum … I didn't want to think about him. He was dead and gone. I didn't let Meggie throw away his letter. I wanted to keep it, to look at it. It made me realise what a fool I was. I was stupid to think that he loved me.

Part of me still wanted to believe that the letter was a bad joke or a mistake. I recognised his writing, he wrote the letter. But did he mean what he said? Did he hate me? Why did he write it? It was like poison, damaging all my memories of him.

I needed to stop thinking about him. Callum didn't love me. He used me to punish my dad. He was even worse than his brother, Jude. It was time to forget him.

I knocked on Jaxon's door and waited.

'Hello,' he said, surprised. 'I wasn't expecting you.'

'You and Meggie were right,' I told him. 'I have to earn some money.'

'We have a booking tomorrow night. Come in and meet the other members of the band.'

He led me through his house to a hut at the bottom of the garden. There was a short, thin boy sitting behind some drums.

'This is Rhino,' said Jaxon. 'And that's Sonny, the keyboard player.'

Sonny was fair-haired, like Jaxon, but big and strong.

'We were practising before you arrived,' Jaxon told me. 'Let's try a song. Do you know *Red to Green*, by Gibson Dell?'

'Yes, I think so,' I replied nervously.

They started to play, but I missed the start of my first line.

'Let's try again,' smiled Jaxon. 'Forget that we're here. Just sing it for yourself.'

I nodded, closed my eyes and started to sing. *Red to Green* is a song that starts softly but gets louder and louder, which I love. Soon I'd forgotten everything but my enjoyment of the song. When I opened my eyes, they were all staring at me.

'Was I very bad?' I asked, after no one said a word.

31

'I think we've found our singer!' Jaxon said.

Then Sonny and Rhino started smiling.

'There's something you need to know,' I said to Jaxon. 'I don't want to use my real name in the band.'

'What's wrong with your name?' Jaxon said quickly. Too quickly.

'If you're hoping to make money from my name, forget it,' I said angrily. 'If anyone asks, I'm Ridan.'

'Ridan? What does that mean?' said Jaxon.

'It means nothing at all,' I told him.

♦

Jude

I read in the newspaper that Cara was in hospital, kept alive by machines. I cashed her cheques in different banks around the city on the same day. She was in hospital, not dead, so the bank had no reason to refuse them. By the end of the week, I had several thousand pounds. Why didn't I feel happier?

It rains all the time, especially at night when I'm alone and lonely and there is not a cloud in the sky. Deep inside me, it feels that I will never see the sun again.

One night, I phoned the hospital.

'Can you put me through to the Special Care Ward, please?' I asked.

'Just a minute,' the nurse said in a bored voice.

Moments later, I was talking to someone else.

'How is Cara Imega?' I asked.

'Are you a member of her family?' the male voice asked.

'Yes, I'm Joshua Imega, her uncle,' I lied.

'She's not doing very well,' the male voice said quietly. 'We can't give you much information over the phone, but you should get here soon.'

'I see,' I said, and put down the phone.

I did nothing for the rest of the weekend. I sat in the flat, watched TV and thought about Andrew Dorn. I had money and some friends in the Freedom Fighters. I wanted to get close to Dorn and make him pay for his betrayal.

Then the news came on the television. News about the hunt for Cara Imega's murderer. Cara had died that morning in hospital.

♦

Sephy

'Sephy, when are we going to talk about that letter?' Meggie asked. 'Callum loved you. Someone forced him to write it.'

I looked at her. Did she really believe that? Of course no one forced him. But my relationship with Callum had ended, so maybe she didn't want us to live with her now.

'Do you want Rose and me to move out? I could go to Mother's,' I said.

'No, of course not. This is your home for as long as you want. Sephy, did you love my son?'

'Of course I did. I only let him touch me because I loved him.' My cheeks were red with embarrassment. I looked away.

'Then why do you believe that letter?' Meggie asked.

'Because Callum wrote it,' I told her. 'He wrote that hateful, hurtful letter and he meant every word.'

Meggie tried to interrupt, but I continued, 'He was in prison – he was going to hang. He blamed me. It's understandable that he hated me.'

'Callum never hated you,' said Meggie.

'Sometimes I think I'm wrong and Callum really did love me. And then I read his letter again …'

'Then stop reading it and destroy it,' Meggie ordered.

I didn't want to listen or argue any more. I went upstairs to feed Rose. Less than a minute later, Meggie knocked on my door.

'Please give me the letter,' she said. 'If you keep it, it will damage you even more. You'll start to believe it …'

'I already believe it,' I told her.

She shook her head sadly and walked away.

Later that night, I stood nervously outside the club where Jaxon's band was playing. I wanted to turn and run away. Jaxon and the other band members were parking the van. There was a line of people, mostly Crosses, outside the doors, so I joined it to keep a place for the others. Two Cross men in black suits were deciding who could go inside.

'Are you alone? You can go in,' one of the men said to me.

I saw Jaxon and the others running towards me. We started to go in together, but one of the guards jumped in front of us.

'It's OK,' I told him. 'We're together.'

'They're not coming in here,' the guard said. '*You* can, but not them. Those are the rules. Maybe you should choose your … friends more carefully.'

'We're playing here tonight,' Jaxon said angrily.

'You'll have to go in through the back door,' the guard replied.

'So we can *sing* here, but we can't enter through the front door?'

'Those are the rules,' the guard said again. 'Are you part of this band?' he asked me.

'Yes, I am,' I said.

'Well, you can come in this way.'

'Let's go to the back, Jaxon,' Rhino said. 'We need this booking – remember?'

Sonny, Rhino and Jaxon walked away without me. I went through the front entrance, but I was very angry.

'Are any other bands singing tonight?' I asked.

'Yes, one other. They've already arrived. They're in the

changing room behind the stage.'

'Where can I find the owner of the club?' I asked, smiling.

They sent me to the owner's office above the bar. I knocked on the door and waited. A few seconds later, the door opened.

'Mr Kosslik?'

'Yes?' said a Cross man in an expensive suit. 'Can I help you?'

'I'm Ridan. I'm with one of the bands that you hired to sing tonight,' I explained.

'Oh yes,' said Mr Kosslik. 'You've got three blankers with you, haven't you?'

I was careful to keep the smile on my face. I replied, 'Yes. That's why I'm here. Can I collect our payment for tonight now?'

'Why?' Mr Kosslik asked. It was an unusual request and he didn't trust me.

'I don't want to work with the band, but I have to start somewhere,' I began. 'When you've heard me, maybe you'll book me to sing without the others.'

'But that doesn't explain why you want the money now,' Mr Kosslik said. 'That's not how I do business.'

'No, not with … blankers. I'm a Cross, I'm not going to run away with your money. I want to tell the band that I'm leaving tonight. If I give them their money immediately, they won't come up here and cause trouble.'

'I see.'

'I really can sing,' I continued. 'Do you want me to sing now to prove it?'

'OK,' he said, and sat back in his chair.

I took a deep breath, smiled at him and started singing. I pretended that I was a famous singer in front of a crowd of admiring people. When I finished, he was smiling at me.

'You have a great voice,' he told me. 'You need a lot of practice, but I'll help you. I'll teach you everything about the music business that you need to know. You won't learn anything with those blankers.'

'Thanks, Mr Kosslick,' I said. 'I'll do my best for you.'

He opened a drawer and threw an envelope of money at me.

'Thank you,' I said. Then I ran out of his office and down the stairs.

I went to the changing room and found the other band – five nought men.

'Hi, I'm Ridan,' I said. 'My band was going to play here tonight, but we've decided to leave.'

'Why?' the tallest nought asked me, surprised.

'Don't you know?' I said. 'The Freedom Fighters have given Mr Kosslik a warning. They're coming here tonight to cause trouble. I'm not going to be anywhere near this place when they start shooting.'

'Are you serious?' one of the other noughts asked.

'Is this something that I'd joke about?' I said as I walked towards the door.

Less than a minute later, they'd picked up their instruments and gone. I watched them leave as Jaxon, Rhino and Sonny came in.

'Where are *they* going?' Jaxon asked.

'Somebody made them a better offer,' I told him. 'Can we sing *Bad Attitude* first? I have a good reason for asking.'

When we got on stage, Rhino started drumming, slowly. I turned to the crowd.

'How are you all feeling?' I called out.

The crowd around the stage cheered. Rhino's drumming was getting faster and Jaxon and Sonny started playing too. I watched the excited crowd and the anger inside me spread through my whole body. I hated everyone in that room at that moment – noughts and Crosses. Why was it so easy to hate?

You can't come here. You can't play there. No mixing. Stay on your own side. Stay in your own area. And I was the same. I hated myself most of all.

I took a deep breath. I had to sing better than I'd ever sung before. So I started to sing. Anger gave me a strong voice and took away my nervousness. I wasn't Sephy any more, I was Ridan, a girl with nothing to lose. When we finished, the crowd was cheering loudly.

'Do you want more?' I shouted.

'Yes!' they screamed back.

For the first time that evening, I stopped smiling. 'Well, it's not going to happen,' I said.

The cheers stopped. The crowd was confused – and the other band members were too.

'When we came here tonight, we were going to sing a lot of songs,' I continued, 'each song bigger and better than the one before. But we weren't allowed to come in through the front door. We were told to go to the back. If we're not good enough to come through the same door as you, we're not good enough to sing to you. So goodbye. Oh, and the other band have already left the building because they were so angry about the way we were treated.'

I walked off the stage. Jaxon and the others had to follow me. People were starting to complain loudly. But if one person in the audience understood the reason for my anger, I'd done well.

'What are you doing?' Jaxon asked. 'We haven't been paid yet.'

'Oh yes we have,' I said. I showed them Kosslik's money. Sonny put it safely in his pocket. 'Shall we go?' I smiled. 'We all go through the same door or we don't go in at all. OK?'

'OK!' agreed Sonny with a smile.

'We'd better leave –'

Before I could continue, Mr Kosslick was standing in front

of me with two of his guards.

'What are you doing?' he asked angrily. 'You were paid to play for me tonight.'

'We did. We played one song,' I told him.

'I want my money back,' said Mr Kosslik. He waved forward one of his guards.

'That's not a good idea,' I warned him as Sonny tried to pull me away from the guard. 'My real name is Persephone Hadley and my dad is the government minister Kamal Hadley. If you hurt any of us, you'll all hang before the end of the week.'

The guard looked uncertainly at Mr Kosslik. Mr Kosslik stared at me and I looked straight back at him. I knew that he believed me.

'Let them go,' he said to the guards. Then he turned back to me. 'But don't ever come back to my club again.'

'Don't worry,' I said. 'We're too good for this place.'

We picked up our equipment and left. Nobody tried to stop us. One or two people even cheered.

'Would your dad really help us?' Jaxon asked when we were outside.

'No,' I said. 'He's on their side.'

A few days later, we had another booking – at a nought club run by a woman called Alice.

Earlier that day, Meggie and I had had our first real argument.

'You can look after Rose while I'm working, can't you?' I said to Meggie.

'I'm not her mother, Sephy,' said Meggie. 'I offered to help, not look after her all the time.'

'Rose is your granddaughter,' I said coldly. 'Callum's child.'

'She's a baby. She needs her mother.'

'I'm here most of the time,' I shouted at her.

Meggie looked at me. 'I know you want to fight with

someone, Sephy, but you're not going to fight with me.'

'Oh, no, I mustn't argue with you, Meggie. You might tell me what you *really* think of me, like Callum did.'

Meggie handed Rose back to me. 'I'm going shopping,' she said coldly. It was our first big disagreement.

I took Rose out for a walk. For the first time I really looked at the world around me. I noticed how poor the area was. There were few trees and the ground was covered with rubbish. Everyone looked tired and no one smiled.

A lot of noughts stared at us. One tall nought woman even turned round and started to follow me. I knew that she was behind me and getting closer. I took a deep breath and turned to face her.

'Can I help you?' I asked coldly. Yes, my story had been in the newspapers, but did that give people the right to insult me in the street?

'I'm sorry, but are you Persephone Hadley?' the woman said. 'You are, aren't you?' She stepped closer, then she smiled. 'I just wanted to say – I admire you.'

She suddenly looked embarrassed and walked away quickly. I wanted to call after her, but she'd disappeared. I smiled and said softly, 'Thank you.' I'd expected her to shout at me. When did I stop trusting people? I smiled at the next nought I walked past. She looked from Rose to me and gave me a look of deep dislike. Right. No more smiling.

After about forty minutes, we went back home. Meggie was still out. Rose started crying and didn't stop. I felt so alone. I needed to think, away from Rose, away from everyone. I wanted to forget about Callum and his letter. I wanted to forget how much I'd loved him.

Later that night, I lay in bed unable to sleep. 'Can you see me Callum?' I whispered. 'Can you see how you've ruined my life? Does that make you laugh or does it make you cry?'

Chapter 6 Sephy Changes and Meggie Is Worried

Sephy

Russell's was the first nought club that I'd ever been to. We entered the place – through the front door – and were greeted by a big, strong woman with red hair and thick make-up.

'Hello,' I said, and held out my hand.

'Aren't you polite?' the woman laughed. She put her arms around me. 'I'm Alice. The audience tonight is a little noisy.'

We went through the club to the changing-room. The place smelled of beer and cigarette smoke. I was the only Cross there and everyone was staring at me. I heard some of them talking about me.

'What's she doing here?'

'Who's the dagger?'

When we walked on to the stage, there was total silence. A crowd of nought men and women stood in front of me, cold and unwelcoming.

'We can do this,' Jaxon whispered in my ear. 'Remember how good you were last time.' He walked back to his microphone and left me in front of the crowd. There was no one to hide me.

I opened my mouth to sing, but my voice failed and there was silence. The music stopped and I stared out into the crowd, who were whispering and laughing. I knew that they hated me.

I remembered other times when people hated me. When I went to Callum's house after his sister's death and was told to leave. When I was beaten in the school toilets because Callum was my friend.

I hadn't changed. Inside I was still the same frightened little girl.

'What are you doing?' Jaxon whispered angrily. 'Sing – or we won't leave this place alive.'

The music started again, but I couldn't hear it because of the shouting from the crowd.

'Go back to where you came from ...'

'Get out of here ...'

'We don't want any daggers in here ...'

Someone threw something small and hard, which hit me in the face.

Jaxon came over to me again. 'We'd better go,' he said and started to take off his guitar.

Blood poured down my cheek. I touched it with my fingers, then slowly spread it across my face. The crowd wanted my blood, so I gave it to them. The noise quietened as I watched them.

'OK, you win. I'll get off the stage,' I shouted. 'But first we're going to sing *Bad Attitude*.'

'Are you crazy?' Jaxon said. 'You can't sing that. This crowd will think that you're singing about them.'

'Play *Bad Attitude* or I'm walking off the stage,' I told him.

He gave me a long, hard look. 'I hope you know what you're doing,' he said.

Moments later, the boys started playing and I started to sing. The crowd hated it, hated me. I stared at them angrily as I finished:

... I guess you'll never learn
With your bad attitude.

But then I thought of Rose, asleep with a smile on her face, and my anger disappeared. Something hit me on the shoulder – the audience were still throwing things at me. Nobody wanted me, except Rose. Rose was the only important thing in the world, now and in the future. Her father was part of my history.

'I have one more song for you,' I said into the microphone. I don't think anyone heard me. 'This song is *Rainbow Child*, for my daughter Rose.'

I started to sing the beautiful words about children and the

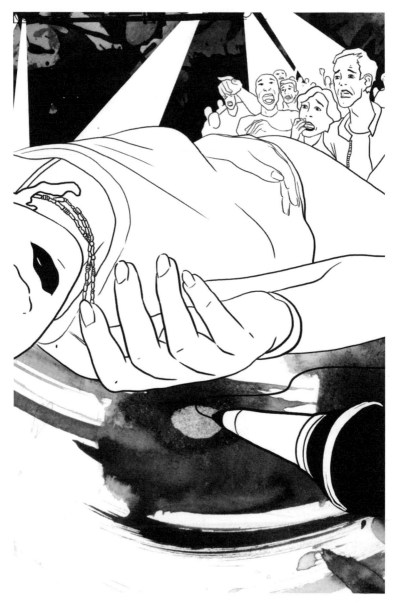

I fell to the floor and everything went black.

hope that they bring to the world. I closed my eyes. I wasn't in Russell's any more, but with my baby.

The song finished and in my mind I was still with her, holding her tightly. I had no life without her. All around me it was quiet. Then, slowly, people started to cheer. Alice stood on the stage, smiling. Jaxon was talking to me, but I couldn't hear him. He looked happy.

I wanted to go home and hold my baby. I needed to pick her up in my arms and never let her go. I turned to Jaxon – and then I fell to the floor and everything went black.

◆

Meggie

Life with Sephy was becoming more and more difficult. We didn't talk much and the evenings were mostly silent. One night, when Callie was asleep in her cot upstairs, I tried to discuss Callum's letter.

'Sephy, you mustn't believe what was in that letter …'

'I've already told you,' Sephy interrupted without looking at me. 'I don't want to talk about it.'

I didn't believe that Callum wrote those hateful, hurtful things. Callum loved Sephy. Sephy didn't understand how much I loved her too. I loved and admired her for having my grandchild.

Every time I looked at Callie Rose, I thought of Callum. She had the same eyes. I wanted to keep her safe, but her life was going to be difficult. She wasn't a nought or a Cross.

I was worried about Sephy. In the past, she'd never let Callie cry in her cot, but after Callum's letter she was slower to go to her baby. One night, when Callie was crying loudly, I went upstairs to her. Sephy was in the bedroom, staring down at the baby. Her face was blank – there was no love in her eyes.

'Is everything all right, Sephy?' I asked, frightened.

She turned to me and smiled with her mouth, not her eyes,

43

and nodded. 'Yes, Meggie. Everything's OK,' she told me.

Every day was worse. Callie cried more often and Sephy didn't want to hold her. She spent as much time as possible out of the house. Finally, I made a decision and phoned Jasmine Hadley.

'Meggie,' she said, when she answered the phone. 'Is my daughter all right? Has something happened?'

'No, Sephy and Callie are both fine,' I said quickly. 'But I'm worried about Sephy. She's not ill, but I'm anxious about her behaviour. It's not something that I can discuss over the phone. Perhaps we can meet?'

'Shall I come to your home tomorrow?'

She came the next day. Holding a sleeping Callie in my arms, I went to open the front door.

'Hello, Mrs Hadley.'

'Hello, Meggie. Hello, Callie dear.' Mrs Hadley kissed Callie's cheek and took her from me.

She came into the hall. 'It's good to see you, Meggie. I've wanted to come and see you many times during the last few years. How's my daughter?'

'She's OK. She fainted last night while she was singing with the band. Jaxon brought her home and she's in bed.'

'She's been doing too much,' said Mrs Hadley. 'She's only just had a baby. Can I see her?'

'I thought we could talk first.'

I took her into the living room and told her everything, including about the letter.

'I see,' she said at last. She looked down at Callie. 'Sephy feels things very deeply. I wasn't a good mother to her. I only thought about my husband and I drank too much. By the time I was ready to care for her and Minerva, I didn't know them. And Sephy is like me. Callum meant everything to her, so his letter ...'

'Callum didn't write that letter,' I interrupted. 'It looks like his writing but he cared too much about Sephy.'

'But Sephy *thinks* he wrote it,' Mrs Hadley said.

'What can we do?' I asked. 'We have to do something. Callie deserves the best care we can give her. I'm worried about the way Sephy's treating her,' I said.

'Why?' Mrs Hadley asked quickly. 'What's she doing?'

'Yes, what *am* I doing, Meggie?' I heard Sephy's cold voice behind me.

I turned round quickly. 'Sephy, I didn't mean …'

'How dare you criticise me!' Sephy said angrily. 'Neither of you understands what I've experienced during the last year. Meggie, you keep saying that Callum didn't write that letter. Well, he did. I know his writing better than I know my own. Mother, you say you'll do anything for Rose. Well, you did nothing for Minerva and me. Rose isn't your second chance to be a mother.'

Both Mrs Hadley and I tried to speak, but Sephy refused to listen.

'Leave me alone, both of you.' Her voice was getting higher and louder. 'I can't please anyone, so now I'm going to please myself.'

She ran out of the room. Mrs Hadley and I looked at each other. A moment later, we heard the front door close noisily.

Something around us had changed for the worse. Could we ever change it back?

Chapter 7   Jude Is Arrested and Meggie Asks for Help

Meggie

Finally, after a month, Sephy started talking to me again. We didn't say much, but it was better than nothing. She was also writing songs and poems, and sometimes she read them to me.

Every day I thought about that hateful letter. I knew that Callum had loved Sephy, but how could I make her believe in his love?

One night we were watching the TV news together when I got a terrible shock.

'*The police are now looking for this man, Jude McGregor, in connection with the murder of Cara Imega. If you see him, please contact the police immediately. He is dangerous and may have a gun.*'

A photo of Jude when he was eighteen appeared on the television. I couldn't speak. Jude, my son, was wanted for murder. It couldn't be true. He wouldn't beat a poor girl to death. Jude didn't do it. *Did he …?*

My son had done many bad things, but he did them for the Freedom Fighters. He was fighting for something that he believed in. But now the police thought he'd killed a girl. They wouldn't stop looking for him until they caught him and hung him.

I started to pray. *Please God, don't let me lose my last child.*

♦

Jude

The night air was very cold. I buttoned my jacket and looked around nervously. There weren't many people in the city centre.

I found a telephone and called my friend Morgan.

'Did you do it?' he asked. 'Did you kill that girl?'

'How many times do I have to say no before you believe me?' I asked angrily.

'You frighten me sometimes. Did you *know* Cara Imega?'

'Maybe,' I replied.

'Do you know who killed her?'

I didn't answer.

'Well, even if you're innocent, stay hidden for the next few months,' said Morgan.

'I know,' I said, annoyed. 'And Morgan – I didn't do it.'

I ended the call. I kept telling myself that I'd done nothing wrong. I'm a Freedom Fighter. Sometimes we have to do what's necessary. But I didn't believe my own words.

The police had given my real name, and a picture of me, to the world. The fingerprints in Cara's house matched the ones that they had of me in their records.

But Cara was in the past and I had to think about the future. I couldn't let the police catch me now. I had too much to do. I still wanted to prove that Andrew Dorn was working for the blankers.

'Hello, Jude …'

At the sound of my name, I turned round. My hand went quickly to the gun in my jacket pocket, but I was too late. At least eight dagger police were surrounding me. I knew what had happened. They'd found me through my call to Morgan. Morgan had betrayed me too. Another one of my rules:

Friends are just people who haven't betrayed you yet.

'PUT YOUR HANDS IN THE AIR! … LIE DOWN ON THE GROUND NOW! WE WON'T TELL YOU AGAIN.'

I knew that I couldn't fight them. I lay down on the ground and immediately four of the daggers jumped on me, pulled my arms behind my back and tied my hands. Someone kicked me in my side. Their hands were searching me. They took both the gun and the knife that I kept in my left sock. I was pushed into the back of a police car with a dagger police officer on each side of me.

'You're going to hang for this,' said the policeman on my left. 'Just like your murdering brother.'

They took me to a police station, where two dagger detectives questioned me. Detective Georgiou, the woman, did most of the talking. The other one, Detective Zork, stayed silent.

47

I remembered my Freedom Fighters' training. Answer questions slowly and keep your answers simple. Only answer the questions that you want to answer.

The questions came quickly: When did you meet Cara Imega? How long have you known her? We found your fingerprints in her house. Were you robbing her when she came in? I didn't say anything except to refuse a lawyer.

Finally Detective Zork spoke. 'We know it was you. We're going to prove that you murdered Cara Imega and then you'll hang.' He was getting angry and that amused me. 'Go back to your cell, McGregor,' he said.

I smiled at him. 'Is your name really Zork? Poor you!'

He punched me so hard in the stomach that I was bent double and coughing.

'Do you still think my name is funny?' asked the dagger.

I straightened up slowly. 'Are you going to stand there and let him hit me?' I asked Georgiou.

'I don't know what you're talking about,' she replied coldly. 'You fell and landed on the back of the chair.'

'And what would you say if he threw me out of the window?' I asked.

'You tried to kill yourself,' Detective Georgiou told me. 'Who knows how the mind of a murderer works?'

We stood in silence. They wanted me to do something so they could punish me. But Mrs McGregor didn't give birth to stupid children.

'Back to your cell, McGregor,' Zork said.

And I replied, 'Yes, sir.'

♦

Sephy

Rose was asleep and I was watching TV when Meggie answered the telephone. When she came back she said, 'Sephy, will you come with me to see Jude? He's just phoned from Baylinn Police Station. The police have arrested him for the murder of Cara Imega. They're moving him to Bellview Prison the day after tomorrow. Will you come and see him with me?'

'I'm the last person that Jude wants to see,' I told Meggie.

'You don't have to talk to him. You can wait for me outside. But I don't want to go into the police station alone.'

I tried to smile. I didn't want to go anywhere near Jude, but Meggie needed my support.

'Of course I'll come with you. But what about Rose? I don't want to take her all the way to Baylinn.'

'I'm sure Mrs Straczynski next door will look after her for an hour or two,' said Meggie. 'Thank you, Sephy. I'm very grateful for your help.'

When we arrived at the police station, I went inside with her and asked to see Jude. The police officer behind the desk stopped smiling when I said Jude's name.

'Who are you?'

'I'm Sephy. And this is Jude's mother, Meggie McGregor.'

'Sephy who?' the officer asked. 'I need your full name.'

'Persephone Mira Hadley,' I replied.

The officer wrote down our names and told us to sit down, then he didn't move for thirty minutes. We watched him help other people with their problems while we waited and waited. Two hours later, I was really angry and I returned to the desk.

'Are you going to let us see Jude McGregor or not?' I said quietly. 'You've kept us waiting long enough.'

'Jude McGregor is an animal,' the officer told me. Then he added in a low voice, 'But his Cross visitors are worse.'

'If you don't let us see him immediately, my family will make sure that you lose your job.'

The officer looked carefully at me and I stared straight back at him. He knew that I was serious.

'Follow me, please,' he said, his voice hard and cold. He led us into an interview room. 'We'll bring Jude McGregor here and an officer will stay in this room at all times.'

When he left I said, 'Meggie, I'll wait for you outside.'

Finally, Meggie came out. I smiled, but she didn't smile back.

'Sephy, I need your help,' she said. 'I need to know what evidence the police have against Jude.'

'The police won't tell me …' I began.

'You know people. Couldn't you find out?'

'But why do you need that information?' I asked.

'Jude says that he's innocent.'

'And you believe him?' I asked.

She didn't answer. We left the police station and walked to the bus stop in silence. Jude was cruel and nasty, but Meggie was his mother.

'Do you think Jude killed Cara Imega?' I tried again.

'He promises he didn't do it …'

'And you believe him?'

Meggie looked straight into my eyes. 'He wouldn't lie to me.' I said nothing. 'Will you help me? Please.'

'I'll try,' I said slowly. 'But I can't promise anything.'

'You'll find out the truth,' Meggie said. 'I know you will.'

Chapter 8   Sephy Uses Minerva and Jude Has a Surprise

Sephy

I sat in Anada's seafood restaurant, waiting for my sister Minerva to arrive. I'd asked her for a meeting and to my surprise she'd agreed. I needed her help.

I looked at the menu. It was an expensive place and I didn't have much money. One of the dishes was called Blanker's Pleasure. I looked around. There were no noughts eating and only one serving the food. How did he feel when someone ordered a Blanker's Pleasure?

'Hello, Sephy. How are you?'

I looked up, then jumped to my feet.

'Hello, Minerva. Thanks for agreeing to meet me.'

We didn't touch or kiss.

'How are you?' she asked. 'How's Callie Rose?'

'Rose is fine,' I replied. 'She's with Meggie at the moment.'

'Could I come to see her some time? I don't want to upset you or Meggie.'

'Why would I be upset?' What did she think I'd do? Kick her down the street? But it was strange that Minerva wanted to visit us.

'Can I order some food for you?' Minerva asked.

'Well, I was only going to have a glass of water,' I began, worried about the cost.

'Don't be silly.' Minerva turned to the waiter and ordered the most expensive dishes. Before the waiter walked away, I asked him, 'Don't you think it's insulting to call a dish Blanker's Pleasure?'

The waiter looked at me suspiciously. 'We've served Blanker's Pleasure for years.'

'Then don't you think it's time the name was changed?' I said.

'Er … I'll get your order,' said the waiter. He didn't want an argument.

'Was that necessary?' Minerva said. 'My newspaper brings a lot of customers here. My boss won't be pleased if we upset the waiters.'

'How can a new reporter afford this place?' I asked.

'I may be a new reporter, but I'm getting better and better

jobs,' Minerva said proudly.

'So have I made trouble for you by complaining about the name of a dish? Don't you think this place should join the twenty-first century like the rest of us? Why don't you write about that? '

'Because my boss will refuse to print it,' said Minerva calmly. 'It's not news. You have to be patient, Sephy. No one can change the world overnight – not even you.'

'We've had centuries to change people's attitudes,' I argued. 'But attitudes are getting worse, not better. When I was shopping with Rose two days ago, three different people asked me whose child she was. When I said mine, one man told me to give her to a blanker family.'

'Don't think about it,' said Minerva.

'That's easy for you to say.' I was going to continue the argument, but I didn't want to spoil Minerva's lunch.

'Have you heard about Jude McGregor's arrest?' asked Minerva. 'How do you feel about that?'

'Are you interviewing me, Minerva?' Minerva stared down at the table. 'You are, aren't you? Is that why you agreed to meet me for lunch?'

'It's my job, Sephy. I need your help. I've got something to ask you and I just want you to listen – OK?' She paused. 'But first, why did you want us to meet?'

'I wanted to talk to you about Jude too,' I said. 'Did he do it? What evidence do the police have against him?'

Minerva looked at me. She was wondering whether to share her information.

'I won't tell the world what you tell me,' I said. 'I have a good reason for asking.'

'I know that Jude McGregor's fingerprints were found in Cara Imega's house. He gave Cara a false name, but the police know it was him. He called himself Steve Winner when he was going out with her –'

'Jude was going out with Cara? A Cross woman? That's impossible!'

'We heard this from a police officer. Several people from Cara's hairdressing salon have recognised Jude, from his picture, as her boyfriend. And after her death, some of her cheques were cashed at banks in the city by a nought man. He wore a hat and sunglasses and kept his head down, but the height and weight match Jude.'

'Did they find any bloody clothing? Any DNA evidence?'

'They didn't find any clothing. Jude isn't stupid. And the scientists are still searching for more DNA evidence.'

I sat back in my chair. 'The fingerprints only prove that he was in Cara's house. They don't prove that he killed her.'

'The police believe that they'll find more evidence.'

'And what does Jude say?' I asked.

'Jude's says that he knew Cara, but nothing more.'

'If the court find him guilty, will he hang?'

Minerva paused. 'I think so.' Then she asked me, 'Why are you so worried about Jude? He shot me and he hates you and your baby. He's dangerous.'

'I want to help Meggie. No one is telling her anything.'

'Stay away from Jude, Sephy,' Minerva warned. 'If you try to help, he'll hurt you. And don't tell anyone about the evidence. It won't make Meggie feel any better.'

'I just want to help her. She's lost two children. If Jude dies, it will kill her.'

'I'm sorry, but if Jude's guilty –'

I interrupted. 'Her other son was innocent but that didn't help him, did it?'

'Sephy, Jude isn't Callum. He tried to kill us – remember? Callum had his faults but –'

'I'm not here to talk about … him,' I said quickly.

Minerva studied me. 'Why is it so hard for you to say Callum's name? If you talk to someone about Callum and ... his death, maybe you can move on with your life. And Meggie can do the same. No one's asking you to forget the past, but you must think about the future.'

How do I do that? I wondered. Every time I looked at my daughter, I saw Callum. She looked more and more like him every day and it frightened me.

'You still haven't told me why you agreed to see me,' I said.

Minerva took a deep breath. 'I'd like an interview with Meggie, for my newspaper. Can you arrange it for me?'

I stared at her. 'Are you crazy? Meggie is having a terrible time – again. How can you ask for an interview?'

'I'll tell her side of the story,' Minerva said. 'Just ask her and let Meggie make the decision.' I began to shake my head. 'It's my job, Sephy. I was shot for you. Do this for me.'

My heart seemed to stop beating when I heard her words: *I was shot for you* ... I said nothing.

'Look, forget what I said.' Minerva shook her head. 'I'm really sorry that I asked. Forgive me?'

'It's OK, Minerva. I'll do what you want. I'll ask Meggie – but that's all I can do. The decision is hers.'

'That's great. Thank you so much.' Minerva smiled happily.

Minerva thought that I could help her get her interview with Meggie. Her job was the most important thing in the world to her. She was using me – but I was also using her. When she found out what I was going to do with her information about Jude, she'd never ask me for anything again.

♦

Jude

'Mr McGregor, I'm on your side – you have to believe that,' said Mr Clooney.

Never trust a Cross. Ever.

'I don't have to believe anything you tell me,' I said coldly. Where had this lawyer come from? He was a stupid old Cross with short white hair and a thin moustache. We were in one of the visitors' rooms in the prison.

'Will you let me advise you? Tell the police that you killed Cara Imega. If you deny it and the court finds you guilty, you'll hang.'

'And if I say I'm guilty?'

'You'll go to prison for twenty-five to thirty years. Afterwards you'll still have some kind of life.'

Twenty-five to thirty years in prison? I'd prefer to hang.

'If that's your best offer, I'm in serious trouble,' I said.

'I'm on your side,' Clooney repeated.

'No, you're not. I don't want you to work for me. I'll defend myself,' I informed him.

Clooney stood up and picked up his papers. He looked down at me and shook his head. 'Do you know what I'm looking at?' he asked quietly.

'No. What?'

'A dead man.'

Later, when I was lying on my bed in my prison cell, the guard told me I had a visitor.

'I don't want to see anyone,' I said angrily.

'Your visitor said that your brother sent her,' said the dagger.

I looked up quickly. Was it Mum? I didn't want to talk to her. I didn't want to watch the hurt on her face as she looked at me. But I couldn't refuse to see her. She was the only family that I had now.

Another dagger guard arrived and they led me to the visitors' room. For criminals like me there were no face-to-face meetings. Instead, a thick glass wall separated the prisoners from visitors.

55

As I sat down, I looked through the glass at my visitor. It wasn't Mum, it was Persephone Hadley. I was shocked – and then angry.

'Hello, Jude,' Sephy said quietly.

'Have you come to laugh at me?'

'No. I've come to save your life.'

I wasn't expecting her to say that. I started to laugh.

'How are you going to do that?' I asked.

She moved closer to me and whispered, 'By giving you an alibi.'

I stopped laughing. Did she really mean it?

'Did you … kill Cara Imega?' Sephy asked. But then she added quickly, 'No, don't answer that. I don't want to know.' I stayed silent. 'How long were you in Cara's house?'

'Why do you need to know?'

Sephy moved closer to the glass. 'If I give you an alibi, are you going to support my story? Or would you prefer to tell the police that I'm lying, and hang?'

'Why are you doing this?'

'For Meggie. If you die, she will too. I can't let that happen.'

'Why not? She means nothing to you.'

'You never believe that you're wrong about anything or anyone,' Sephy said. 'I feel sorry for you.'

'I don't want your pity,' I said angrily.

'Calm down,' Sephy said quietly.

'Do you still dream about my brother?' I asked her suddenly. I wanted to hurt her.

'We're not here to talk about your brother,' Sephy said. She looked at the guards, checking that they couldn't hear her. 'This is what we'll do. You can't deny visiting Cara's house because of your fingerprints. You were there, I arrived, and we left together. Cara was alive when we left. You cashed the cheques because she gave them to you. The police can't prove that she didn't.'

'You'll go to court and lie for me? You'll go to prison if they find out.' I didn't believe she'd do it.

'We'll make the public doubt the police story. They won't take you to court.'

'Nobody will believe that we left the house together,' I told her. 'Everyone knows how much I hate you. I shot your sister!'

'Nobody knows about the shooting except you, me and Minerva. She won't say anything. And yes, we hate each other. But that's why we agreed to meet that night. We wanted to work together to prove that your brother was innocent. We agreed to meet at Cara's. You introduced me to her, but we left almost immediately.'

'The police won't let me go unless they can arrest someone else,' I told her. And then I had an idea. For my idea to work, I had to trust Sephy. I didn't want to trust her, but I had no choice.

'Would you go to the police with this alibi?' I asked carefully.

'No, I'd go to the newspapers. Then when you go to court to say you're innocent, there'll be cameras and reporters around you. They'll want your side of the story. You can talk about your alibi then.'

'How do I know I can trust you?'

'You don't,' she said immediately. 'I hate you, Jude, and I don't want to help you. I'm doing this for Meggie. And I want your promise that afterwards you'll leave me and my daughter alone. I don't want to see you, hear you or think about you again.'

Visiting time was ending. The guards were reminding everyone that they had to leave in a minute.

'Do you agree to my plan or not?' Sephy asked impatiently.

'How will it help you if I agree?' I asked.

'I'll have peace of mind,' Sephy said quietly.

I couldn't let that happen. I moved forward in my chair and whispered, 'But you know that I killed that dagger woman.'

For the first time, Sephy looked away, unable to meet my eyes.

I thought: *Live or die, one way or another, I'll punish you, Sephy Hadley. That's a promise.*

Chapter 9 Jude Talks and Sephy Fears for the Future

Sephy

The doorbell rang. 'I'll answer it,' I called upstairs. Meggie was in her room and didn't open the door now. There were too many photographers outside the house.

It was Minerva. 'Can I come in?' she asked.

I stepped to one side of the door and she walked in.

'Sephy, who is it?' Meggie called from upstairs.

'My sister.'

'Oh.' Meggie appeared at the top of the stairs, looking old and tired.

'Hello, Meggie.' Minerva smiled up at her. 'How are you?'

'OK.' Meggie nodded. 'Can I get you a cup of tea or coffee?'

'I'll have a cup of coffee, please – if it's no trouble,' Minerva said.

When Meggie went into the kitchen, I had an unpleasant thought. 'Minerva, if you try to interview Meggie now, I'll throw you out of the house,' I said angrily. 'What do you want?'

Before she could answer, Meggie came in carrying three cups.

Minerva sat down in a chair. 'Won't you join us, Meggie? I was in the area and wanted to see my niece.'

'She's upstairs asleep,' I told her.

We sat uncomfortably in silence for a few moments, then Minerva spoke.

'Meggie, I was sorry to hear about what happened to Jude.'

'Thank you,' said Meggie.

'It must be hard. Have your neighbours supported you?' my sister asked.

Meggie laughed. 'The neighbours don't speak to us. But 'Sephy's fighting for me,' she said. 'I don't know what I'd do without her.'

'Oh yes?' Minerva said suspiciously. 'How are you helping, Sephy?'

'In any way I can,' I said.

'So you think Jude's innocent?' Minerva asked me thoughtfully.

Meggie answered. 'He told me that he didn't do it,' she said. 'My boy wouldn't lie to me.'

'Have you seen Jude?' Minerva asked.

'Yes, we went last week when he was still in the police station,' Meggie replied.

'Both of you?' Minerva asked quickly.

'Sephy went with me.' Meggie smiled at me. 'Then Sephy went to see Jude in prison a couple of days ago. She's been wonderful …'

'Are you enjoying your job at the *Daily Shouter*, Minerva?' I interrupted. 'It must be hard working your way up as a journalist.'

'Minerva, I didn't know you were a journalist at the *Daily Shouter*,' Meggie said quietly.

'Yes, she got the job a few months ago,' I told Meggie.

'You didn't tell me that,' said Meggie. She gave me a strange

59

look. She was wondering why I hadn't told her.

'I'm sure you have to leave now,' I said to my sister.

'Oh I –' Minerva began. Then she saw my face, 'Yes, I do have another appointment.'

I led the way to the front door.

'Thanks for nothing,' Minerva whispered angrily.

'I told you that you couldn't interview Meggie,' I said.

'I only wanted to ask a few questions,' said Minerva.

As usual, my sister couldn't understand that she was doing anything wrong.

She walked past me without a word and I closed the door loudly behind her. I turned round and Meggie was standing in the living-room doorway, watching me.

'Meggie, do you trust me?' I asked.

She waited a little too long before she answered. 'Yes, I do.'

I knew that she didn't. Maybe Meggie was like me, always waiting for people to hurt her. Always hoping for the best but expecting the worst. Maybe, like me, she was too hurt to believe in anyone or anything.

I felt guilty that I'd broken my promise to Minerva about the interview with Meggie. I'd used my sister because I'd owed that to Meggie. And because of me, Jude might be freed.

I'd already contacted three different newspapers – although not the *Daily Shouter*. Two refused to see me. The third interviewed me, but hadn't printed the story. I'd phoned the local radio station and given an interview, but they hadn't broadcast it.

The silence was good. I wanted to forget about Jude. I didn't want to help a murderer – but I didn't want Meggie to be hurt either. I already felt responsible for the death of one of her sons.

That night, Rose was asleep upstairs and I was watching television. Suddenly I saw Jude being led out of the prison, surrounded by journalists. I started to shake with fear.

'Jude, how are you feeling? Are you guilty?' the reporters asked.

He turned to the crowd of reporters with their TV cameras and microphones. What was he going to do now?

'I'd like to say one thing,' Jude began. 'I didn't kill Cara Imega. I'm completely innocent. Yes, I did know her – she was a good friend – but Persephone Hadley, the daughter of Kamal Hadley, knows I didn't kill Cara. Yes, I was at Cara's house that night, but Sephy and a friend of hers came for me. Cara was alive when Sephy and I left Cara's house. We were together until the early hours of the next morning – so I'm not Cara's killer.' Jude turned to look straight at the TV cameras. 'Sephy, please come forward and tell the authorities the truth. You can't let me hang for something that I didn't do.'

I felt sick. Jude lied so well. And who was this 'friend' who, he said, went with me to Cara's house?

'What did you and Sephy do when you left Cara Imega's house?' a reporter asked.

'We talked – mostly about my brother, Callum,' Jude said. 'We both know he's innocent, and we want to prove it. You Crosses want to destroy my whole family.'

'Is Persephone Hadley your alibi, Jude?'

'Yes, she is. She knows that I didn't murder Cara.'

'Why do you think she hasn't talked to the police?'

'I honestly don't know. Maybe she's protecting her friend.'

'Jude, do you know who *did* kill Cara?'

'Yes, I do. It was the man that Sephy brought to Cara's house. His name's Andrew Dorn. He stayed in the house to make a phone call after we left. Cara was happy for him to use her phone. Andrew Dorn should be in prison, not me.'

'Are you sure it was him?'

'Yes. Sephy told me that Andrew Dorn works secretly for her

father. And I've just learned that he's not only a member of the Freedom Fighters, but one of its leaders. He's working for both sides, but I don't know why he killed Cara. Maybe she heard something when he was on the phone. But *he* did it, not me.'

The reporters were clearly shocked – and I was too. Cleverly, Jude had managed to arrange Dorn's death. My father couldn't use him now and the Freedom Fighters would kill him for his betrayal of them. Jude had also made me look like a coward.

'Is Andrew Dorn working for the Freedom Fighters and betraying the government?' Jude asked. 'Or is he working for the government and betraying the Fighters? I don't know. But I do know that he killed Cara. They can't hang me for something that I didn't do.'

Guards pushed Jude into a prison van, and a shocked TV reporter turned to the camera.

'So Jude McGregor says that he did not murder Cara Imega. The police will, no doubt, now be searching for Andrew Dorn –'

I turned off the TV. The sound of my fear, of my beating heart, was deafening. I wanted to deny everything – but then I remembered my phone calls to the three newspapers and the radio station. My story was almost the same as Jude's. With my help, Meggie wasn't going to lose another son. But with my help, Cara Imega's murderer was going to escape and Andrew Dorn was going to die.

♦

Jude

Happy days are here again! They no longer think that I killed … that Cross woman. And Luke, another member of the Freedom Fighters, has told me that the group will welcome me back. I feel like I've been invited home again. And it's great.

They're not letting me out of prison, though. I've been

found guilty of belonging to the Freedom Fighters, which means two years in prison. But with good behaviour, I'll be out in six to eight months. Even the thought of a few more months in here doesn't worry me. I bought the *Daily Shouter* this morning and the front page has made me smile so much that my lips are aching.

Andrew Dorn is dead. The police believe that he was shot in the back of the head by a Freedom Fighter. Now, when I get out of here, I can think about killing Sephy and her daughter.

It's hard to believe that Sephy's living with my mum – I saw them together on the TV – but with all these news reports, she'll soon move away. She doesn't have any friends on either side. The Crosses blame her for giving an alibi to a nought accused of the murder of a Cross. They think that she's betrayed her own people. The noughts hate her for not giving me an alibi sooner.

Reporters and TV cameras are camped outside my mum's front door, demanding an interview. Sephy hasn't said a word, but she doesn't need to. She gave newspaper and radio interviews before I told my story. She never said anything about Andrew Dorn, of course, but that's not important. The reporters believe she knew him and left him at Cara's house. Then she kept quiet after Cara's death.

You're going to suffer, Sephy. This is just the start.

I hope you're proud of me, Callum. I did it all for you.

Andrew Dorn has been punished for betraying us. And Sephy's alone and hated by everyone. When I come out of prison, I can really punish her.

♦

Sephy

'Do you like this, Rose?' She made a funny noise. 'I agree,' I said, and put the orange dress back on the shelf. We were

63

shopping for clothes because she was growing fast. We hadn't been out together for a long time. I didn't want to go out into the world when Cara Imega's photo was in every newspaper. I couldn't forget that I'd helped her murderer.

I held Rose tightly and kissed the top of her head.

'You're Persephone Hadley, aren't you?'

I turned round, then was sorry I had.

'It is you, isn't it?' said the middle-aged woman behind me, her voice full of hate. 'Thanks to you, that murderer Jude McGregor won't be punished for killing one of us. Blanker-lover.'

I tried to walk away, but she took hold of my arm. Other people had recognised me and were moving closer.

'That's her …'

'Kamal Hadley's daughter …'

'Is that Callum McGregor's baby? You know, the terrorist they hanged …?'

'My husband is a policeman,' the woman said. 'He says that everyone knows Jude McGregor killed that girl. But because of your lies, they can't prove it.'

'Do you really hate your own people so much?' a Cross man asked me.

'I feel sorry for that child,' said another, pointing at Rose.

I started to walk away, but they were all around me. 'Excuse me,' I said to the police officer's wife.

She didn't move, so I pushed past her.

'Blanker-lover.'

'It's OK, baby,' I whispered to Rose. 'It's OK.'

But it wasn't OK. My tears fell on her hair. They were right. What kind of mother was I? I couldn't protect Rose and make her happy. Rose deserved to be happy. How could she be happy with me?

Chapter 10   Another Death?

Jasmine

'Sephy, listen to me,' I said. 'You must stop punishing yourself.'

'Yes, Mother.' Her voice was flat and dead, like the look in her eyes.

'Sephy, come home with me. I don't mean to live. I know you want to stay with Meggie. But come for a few days. I can protect you from the reporters and the TV cameras. They won't get past the guards at my house.'

'You can't protect me from people's opinions, Mother,' said Sephy sadly. 'Most people think that Jude murdered Cara, and thanks to me, he's free.'

'I don't care what other people think,' I told her. 'I'm worried about you and Callie Rose. Are you all right?'

Sephy shook her head. 'No, but I will be.'

I wasn't so sure. Sephy was always such a fighter, but now she looked so tired.

'How's Minerva?' Sephy asked. 'Does she hate me?'

'She's a bit upset,' I said carefully. 'But that will pass.'

'Did she tell you why she's angry with me?'

'Not really. She said she told you something privately and you used it. Against her?'

'I didn't use it against *her*,' Sephy said. 'I hurt *myself* by using her information. Did I get her into trouble?'

'She still has her job. Nobody is certain where your information came from. But her boss asked some searching questions. Minerva's afraid that she won't get another front page story for a long time.'

'Can I tell you something?' Sephy said after a long pause.

'I'm listening.'

'I ... I love you, Mother. You know that, don't you?' Sephy said unexpectedly.

Tears filled my eyes. When they cleared, I saw that Sephy was smiling at me. She was looking at me very carefully. I don't know how to explain that look. It felt that she was saying goodbye.

'Sephy, my love, please let me help you,' I said.

'No, Mother. You can't do anything for me now,' said Sephy softly. 'No one can.'

She's hurting so much and I don't know how to help her. And I'm afraid. Minerva's always been the strong one; Sephy feels everything so deeply.

I blame Callum for all her difficulties. He tricked Sephy into meeting him so he could kidnap her with his Freedom Fighter friends. He said he loved her, but he hurt her. Now everyone hates her and she can't leave the house. And it's all because of Callum. I love my granddaughter very much – but I love my daughter too. Now her eyes are always full of pain and I can't do anything to help.

I'd like to murder Jude McGregor for what he's done to Sephy and his niece. I know everything he said about Sephy was a lie. But why doesn't she defend herself? What power does he have over her?

I've tried to phone Kamal about Sephy, but he's busy with his new wife and family. I don't care about my own feelings – he can't hurt me now. But how can he refuse to help his daughter?

Sephy needs help. I can only show her how much I care. Why didn't I do that sooner?

♦

Meggie

I'm so worried about Sephy. Since the scene in the shopping centre, she's been very quiet. The look on her face frightens me. She's so sad that it breaks my heart.

Jaxon came to the house yesterday afternoon with Sonny and Rhino. I knew immediately that they were bringing bad news.

'Sephy, can we talk to you?' asked Sonny.

Sephy took them into the living room and I followed. She moved to the window and stood there with Callie in her arms. In the sunlight she looked so beautiful.

Rhino put a hand on her shoulder. 'Sephy, I want you to know that this isn't my idea,' he said softly.

Sephy turned to face Jaxon and Sonny. 'Do you have something you want to say, Jaxon?' she asked.

'Sephy, we can't have you in the band any more. No one will book us if you're our singer.'

Sephy didn't say a word.

'It's only for a few months,' said Sonny, his face red with embarrassment. 'Maybe you could practise with us. We could still see you … We still … I still want you … with us.'

'But not enough to support me,' said Sephy quietly. 'Don't worry, I understand.'

'When people have started to forget, you can come back,' Jaxon said, rather anxiously.

'Could you all leave now, please?' said Sephy. 'I'm very tired.'

She turned away and looked out of the window again. I immediately moved forward to show the cowards out of my house.

'She won't let us explain,' Jaxon said to me in the hall.

'Sephy and I understand perfectly,' I told him. 'Now Sephy knows who her friends are.'

'You have to understand our problem,' said Sonny.

'No, I don't. You didn't even ask Sephy for the truth.'

Sonny looked ashamed. Jaxon just looked angry and uncomfortable.

'You can all leave my house now,' I said. 'And don't come back.'

They walked out in silence and I shut the door loudly. Newspaper and magazine reports have attacked poor Sephy. Her mother's told her to be strong. But Sephy refuses to discuss her thoughts and feelings.

This morning, I asked, 'Sephy, when are we going to sit down and talk about Jude?'

'Your son isn't going to hang for Cara Imega's murder. What else can I say?' Sephy asked.

After that, she didn't speak. She stared down at Callie with a strange, blank look on her face,

I'm worried. I'm more than worried – I'm frightened.

◆

Sephy

Dearest Rose,

You're so lovely. Too lovely for this world. You deserve better. You deserve more. I've dressed you in my favourite of all your dresses. My mother bought it for you and the cream material looks beautiful against your light brown skin. Meggie has gone shopping and we're alone in the house. I smile as I watch you. I can't believe that I've made something so perfect.

'I love you, Rose. I want you to be happy,' I whisper. 'It's what you deserve.'

If people left us alone, we could both be happy. But that's never going to happen. The world is no place for someone as beautiful as my baby.

I take you downstairs to the living room. You start to cry a little. I kiss the top of your head, your nose and lips.

'Your mum loves you very much. More than life itself,' I whisper in your ear. 'It's my birthday today, Rose. I want to make it a special day, just for you.'

The song *Rainbow Child* is playing on the radio. I smile at you, you smile at me. I hold you as close to my heart as I can. You begin to cry again because I'm holding you too tightly. But I can't let you go. I don't know how.

I start to sing with the radio, very softly.

Take a look
Stop and stare
Love is shining
Everywhere.
There is nothing
Left to fear,
I am with you
Always near ...

When I stop singing, you've stopped crying. You're so quiet, Rose, so very quiet.

Meggie comes into the room with her shopping bags. I can't see her clearly because of the tears in my eyes. I try to stand up, but my legs don't work. I look down at you. You're so quiet, so peaceful. That's what I want for you. Peace.

'Meggie,' I whisper. 'What should I do? Rose isn't breathing ...'

♦

Meggie

I run to Callie and pull her out of Sephy's hands. Callie's warm, but she's not moving.

For a moment I'm so shocked that I can't speak or think. Callie ... I have to make her breathe again.

I place my mouth over Callie's nose and open mouth and breathe gently. I don't want to do more harm than good to her little body. My hands are shaking with fear. I move my face and breathe in air through my mouth, then I cover Callie's mouth and nose again. *Breathe out. Slowly, gently.*

I place two fingers on her chest and press slowly and regularly. Press for three counts, breathe for three counts. Press for three counts, breathe for three counts. Am I doing the right thing? I don't know.

I need to call an ambulance, but there's no time.

I pray, 'You can do it, Callie, love. Breathe, please breathe.'

'Is she going to be all right?' Sephy whispers.

I turn to her, screaming, 'Sephy, what have you done? WHAT HAVE YOU DONE?'

Sephy looks at me and starts to cry. I don't care about her. I turn away from her. If I look at her, I'll kill her.

'Is she going to be all right?' Sephy shouts. 'Is my baby going to be all right?'

I continue breathing into Callie's nose and mouth, trying to force life back into her.

Callie Rose, breathe for me, love.

Beside me Sephy makes a strange sound. She stares at her daughter with the saddest look on her face. Was that noise the sound of her heart breaking? I hope so.

'Go and phone for an ambulance,' I tell Sephy.

She doesn't hear me. She looks at Callie without a word. But silent tears keep falling down her cheeks.

'Take a breath, Callie,' I whisper. 'Don't give up.'

Callum, I think, *if you ever loved Sephy, if you love your daughter, bring her back to us. Please bring her back.*

'Sephy, what have you done?'

Callie Rose, breathe for me, love.

Breathe …

BREATHE …

Breathe …

ACTIVITIES

Chapter 1–2

Before you read

1 Look at the Word List at the back of the book. Check the meanings of words that are new to you. Then use forms of the words below in these sentences.

accuse alibi arrest authorities band betray cash cell cheer cot evidence hang lawyer pray pregnant punch suspicious trust truth

   a The police ..... Mr Jones because they had ..... that he had ..... Mr Smith in the face.

   b 'You say you have an .....? You were with your wife?' said the policeman. 'Are you sure that you're telling the .....?'

   c When she found that she was ....., she bought a ..... for her baby.

   d He ..... his friend, but the friend ..... him and took all the money.

   e She told her ..... that the police were ..... her of murder.

   f The audience ..... when the ..... came on stage.

   g He ..... every night in his small prison ..... that the ..... would not ..... him.

   h There was something ..... about the woman who ..... the cheques.

2 *Knife Edge* continues the story that began in the book *Noughts and Crosses*. Read the Introduction to this book carefully. Then use these words to describe relationships between the main characters.

   wife   sister   brother   parents   girlfriend   mother

   a Meggie McGregor is Jude, Callum and Lynette's ..... .

   b Jasmine Hadley is (or was) Kamal Hadley's ..... .

   c Minerva is Sephy Hadley's ..... .

   d Sephy was Callum McGregor's ..... .

   e Sephy and Callum are Callie Rose's ..... .

   f Jude McGregor is Callum McGregor's ..... .

3 Discuss these questions with another student.
   a Why can't noughts and Crosses live together peacefully?
   b Which three members of the McGregor family have died? Why?
   c Why is Jude McGregor hiding from the authorities?
   d Who is Andrew Dorn, and why is he important to both the noughts and the Crosses?
   e Why does Jude hate Sephy so much?

While you read
   4 Who:
   a betrayed the Freedom Fighters?   ....
   b is running from the police with Jude?   ....
   c helps them to escape?   ....
   d has just had a baby?   ....
   e dislikes Sephy because of the colour of her skin?   ....
   f died before his child was born?   ....
   g sees Jude outside her house?   ....
   h meets Jude in a bar?   ....
   i is moved to a special ward in the hospital?   ....

After you read
   5 Discuss how Jude feels about each of these people. Give reasons for your opinions.
   a Andrew Dorn
   b Dylan Hoyle
   c Sephy Hadley
   d Meggie McGregor
   e Cara
   6 What do you feel about Jude? Make a list of the things that he does in the first two chapters of the book. Do you think that he is simply a bad man and a criminal, or can you understand his activities and ideas? Does he do anything that makes you like or admire him?

Chapter 3–4

Before you read

7 Discuss these questions.

    a Will Jude see Cara again? Why? What does he want from the relationship? How do you think she feels about him?

    b What do you know about Sephy's home life? Where was she living before she had her baby? Where will she go when she leaves the hospital?

    c In Chapter 4 someone is badly hurt. Who do you think it is? Why do you think they get hurt?

    d Sephy receives a letter that affects her very badly. It makes her think again about her love for Callum and their child. Who do you think the letter is from?

While you read

8 Complete each sentence with the endings below. Write 1–8.

    a Jude sees Cara because ...   .

    b Cara sees Jude because ...   .

    c Minerva asks Sephy to move ...   .

    d Roxie's brother Jaxon ...   .

    e Jude hits Cara because ...   .

    f Sephy upsets her mother ...   .

    g Minerva gets a job as ...   .

    h A prison guard brings Sephy ...   .

       1) back to their family home.

       2) he wants her money.

       3) plays the guitar and sings.

       4) she falls in love with him.

       5) a reporter on the *Daily Shouter*.

       6) by moving into Meggie's house.

       7) an upsetting letter from Callum.

       8) he is afraid of his feelings for her.

After you read

9 Choose the correct words.

    a When Sephy was pregnant, Jude shot *her / Minerva* in

the arm.

b When Jaxon gets angry with Nurse Solomon, he calls her a *Cross / dagger*.

c Jasmine Hadley stopped drinking *before / when* Callum was killed.

d Jude meets Cara regularly for two *weeks / months*.

e After he hits her, he takes her *money / keys*.

f Sephy moves into Meggie's house in a *Cross / nought* area.

g Jaxon asks Sephy to *sing / play* with his band.

h In his letter, Callum tells Sephy that he *loves / hates* her.

10 Work with another student. Have this conversation.

Student A: You are Sephy. Both your mother and Meggie McGregor have asked you to move in with them. You have to make a decision about where to live. Discuss your choices with Roxie.

Student B: You are Roxie, in the same hospital ward as Sephy. You see that Sephy is upset and ask her about her problems. Help her to make a decision by discussing her choices.

Chapter 5–6

Before you read

11 Look at the title of Chapter 5, and discuss these questions:

a Why does Sephy change her mind about joining the band?

b What news will Jude hear, and how will it affect him?

While you read

12 Are these sentences right (✓) or wrong (✗)?

a Sephy believes that the letter is from Callum.   .....

b She uses her real name in Jaxon's band.   .....

c Jude isn't interested in Cara's condition.   .....

d Cara dies.   .....

e Meggie doesn't believe that Callum hated Sephy.   .....

f The band's first booking is at a Cross club.   .....

g Sephy tricks the club owner because she's angry with him.   .....

h The crowd likes Sephy's singing.   .....

i The band's second booking is also at a
Cross club.   .....

j The audience throw things at Sephy and hurt her. .....

k Jasmine phones Meggie because she's worried
about Sephy.   .....

After you read

13 Who is speaking? Who to? Who or what are they talking
about?

a 'Was I very bad?'

b 'If anyone asks, I'm Ridan.'

c 'She's not doing very well.'

d 'Someone forced him to write it.'

e 'I already believe it.'

f 'They're not coming in here.'

g 'Is this something that I'd joke about?'

h 'She's a baby. She needs her mother.'

i 'What's she doing here?'

j 'Is my daughter all right?'

14 Imagine that you are Sephy. Think about your answers to
these questions. Then explain your feelings to other students.

a Why do you believe what Callum wrote in the letter?

b How does the letter make you feel about Callum?

c How does it make you feel about your daughter?

d Why are you now calling your daughter Rose instead
of Callie?

Chapters 7–8

Before you read

15 What do you think will happen in the next two chapters?
Discuss these questions with another student.

a Will the police catch Jude?

b Will Sephy continue to sing with the band?

c Will she continue to live with Meggie?

16 Put these sentences in the right order. Number them 1–8.

a The police search for Cara's murderer. .....

b Jude decides to defend himself in court. .....

c Meggie and Sephy's relationship improves. .....

d Meggie and Sephy go to the police station. .....

e Sephy offers to give Jude an alibi. .....

f Minerva asks for an interview with Meggie. .....

g The police catch Jude. .....

h Sephy asks Minerva about the evidence
against Jude. .....

After you read

17 Discuss why these are important in the story.

a Jude's phone call to Morgan

b fingerprints

c a dish called Blanker's Pleasure

d cheques cashed in banks in the city

e an alibi

18 Imagine that you are Sephy. Meggie asks you to help her get information about the evidence against Jude. You will have to visit Jude at the police station. How do you feel? Do you want to see Jude? Why (not)? Why do you want to help Meggie?

19 Discuss Sephy's decision to give Jude an alibi. How does she do it? Can you understand her reasons? Can you defend what she does? Give reasons for your opinions.

Chapter 9–10

Before you read

20 Look at the titles of the next two chapters and discuss these questions.

a Who do you think Jude will talk to if he is freed? Why will this make Sephy afraid for the future?

b There is a question mark after the title of Chapter 10. Why? Who do you think might die at the end of this book?

21 How do you *want* this story to end? What do you want to happen to:

    a   Jude?

    b   Sephy?

    c   Callie Rose?

    d   Minerva?

While you read

22 Circle the correct answers

    a   Who believes that Jude didn't kill Cara?

        Minerva   Sephy   Meggie

    b   Who wants to ask Meggie questions about Jude?

        Jasmine   Minerva   Sephy

    c   Who accuses Andrew Dorn of killing Cara?

        Sephy   Jude   Meggie

    d   Who is killed by a Freedom Fighter?

        Jude   Morgan   Andrew Dorn

    e   Who is hated by both the noughts and the Crosses?

        Sephy   Meggie   Kamal Hadley

    f   Who takes Callie Rose shopping?

        Meggie   Sephy   Jasmine

    g   Who wants Sephy to move into her house?

        Meggie   Minerva   Jasmine

    h   Who wants Sephy to leave the band?

        Jaxon   Rhino   Sonny

    i   Who tries to save Callie Rose's life?

        Meggie   Sephy   Jasmine

After you read

23 Answer these questions.

    a   Why does Minerva visit Meggie and Sephy?

    b   Why is Sephy angry about Minerva's visit?

    c   How has Sephy used Minerva?

    d   How does Jude explain Cara's death when he speaks to reporters?

    e   Why does Sephy feel guilty about helping Jude?

    f   Why are the people in the shopping centre angry with Sephy?

    g   Why does Jasmine ask Sephy to come home with her?

h Why does Jaxon want Sephy to leave the band?

24 Work with another student.

Student A: You are Meggie. Talk to Jasmine Hadley about your fears for Sephy and Callie Rose (before the end of the story). What do you think could happen to them?

Student B: You are Jasmine. Discuss Meggie's fears and ask questions about what has happened to them. Suggest how you can help your daughter and granddaughter.

25 Is Callie Rose dead? *Knife Edge* is the second book about the Hadley and McGregor families. The third book, *Checkmate*, continues their stories. Do you think that Callie Rose appears in the next book? Discuss your thoughts with other students and give reasons for your answers.

Writing

26 You are Jude and you are hiding from the authorities with Morgan. You haven't talked to your mother for months, but you want to write a letter to her. Tell her about your life with the Freedom Fighters and why you can't visit her. Describe how you feel about her.

27 When she is in hospital, Sephy writes letters to her daughter Callie Rose. She uses these letters to explain her thoughts and feelings and to describe the world around them. Write a letter to a child telling them about *your* life. Describe how and where you live and what is important to you.

28 Write a conversation between Cara Imega and a friend about the young man, Steve, that Cara has met. Cara explains where and how they met and why she likes him. The friend asks questions to get as much information as possible about this new boyfriend.

29 Write a letter or an email to the restaurant where Minerva and Sephy meet. Explain why the name Blanker's Pleasure should not be used on the menu.

30 You are Detective Georgiou and you want to question Jude about Cara Imega's death. You are sure that Jude is the murderer but you must prove it. Write ten questions that you want to ask Jude after his arrest.

31 You are a newspaper reporter. You were outside the police station when Jude talked about Cara Imega's death. Write a report about what he said, and explain what will happen to him next. Include the background to Jude's arrest and a short interview with Detective Georgiou.

32 Write a telephone conversation between Sephy and Minerva. Sephy wants to explain why she gave Jude an alibi and used Minerva's information about fingerprints and DNA. Will Minerva understand and forgive her?

33 Look at the words of the song *Rainbow Child*. What is the song about? Do the words make you feel happy and hopeful, or sad? Now write your own song about something that is important to you. It could be a song about love and about friendship, or something in your society that you feel strongly about.

34 What happens next? Does Callie Rose live or die? You have already discussed your thoughts with other students. Now write twenty to thirty lines of the next part of the story. You can decide what happens, but your chapter opening should follow immediately from the end of this book.

35 Did you enjoy this book? Did you find it interesting? Do you think it succeeds in mixing politics with the story of the Hadley and McGregor families? Would you advise other people to read it? Why (not)? Write a report about the book for a magazine or newspaper.

WORD LIST

accuse (v) to say that you believe someone is guilty of a crime or of doing something bad

alibi (n) something that proves a person was not where a crime happened, and therefore is not the criminal

arrest (n/v) the act of taking someone to a police station because the police think he or she has done something illegal

audience (n) a group of people who watch and listen to a public performance

authorities (n pl) a group of people – the government and/or the police, for example – who hold power in a society

band (n) a group of musicians, especially ones who play popular music

betray (v) to be disloyal to your friends or your country so you harm or upset them; this is **betrayal**

blank (adj) showing no emotion, understanding or interest

cash (v) to exchange a cheque for the amount of money written on it

cell (n) a small room in a prison or police station where prisoners are kept; a small group of people who are working secretly as part of a larger political organisation

cheek (n) one of the soft, round parts of your face below your eyes

cheer (n/v) a shout of support or happiness

cot (n) a small bed with high sides for a baby or young child

DNA (n) material in the human body (and in animals and plants) that causes people's physical characteristics and can affect their personalities and abilities. The police can match *DNA* (from skin or hair, for example) left at the scene of a crime with a criminal.

evidence (n) facts or signs that show clearly that something exists or is true

freedom (n) the right to do what you want without being controlled by anyone

hang (v) to kill someone by tying something around their neck and taking the support away from under their feet

lawyer (n) someone who has studied the law, tells people about it, and can speak for them in court